W0044139

# IN PRAISE OF HERESY

# IN PRAISE OF HERESY

*From Socrates to Ambedkar*

## RAMIN JAHANBEGLOO

OXFORD
UNIVERSITY PRESS

# OXFORD
UNIVERSITY PRESS

Oxford University Press is a department of the University of Oxford.
It furthers the University's objective of excellence in research, scholarship,
and education by publishing worldwide. Oxford is a registered trademark of
Oxford University Press in the UK and in certain other countries.

Published in India by
Oxford University Press
22 Workspace, 2nd Floor, 1/22 Asaf Ali Road, New Delhi 110002, India

© Oxford University Press, 2021

The moral rights of the author have been asserted.

First edition published in 2021

All rights reserved. No part of this publication may be reproduced, stored in
a retrieval system, or transmitted, in any form or by any means, without the
prior permission in writing of Oxford University Press, or as expressly permitted
by law, by licence, or under terms agreed with the appropriate reprographics
rights organization. Enquiries concerning reproduction outside the scope of the
above should be sent to the Rights Department, Oxford University Press, at the
address above.

You must not circulate this work in any other form
and you must impose this same condition on any acquirer.

ISBN-13 (print edition): 978-0-19-013054-1
ISBN-10 (print edition): 0-19-013054-7

ISBN-13 (eBook): 978-0-19-099295-8
ISBN-10 (eBook): 0-19-099295-6

Typeset in Berling LT Std 10.5/16.5
by Transistics Data Technologies, Kolkata 700 091
Printed in India by Rakmo Press, New Delhi 110 020

*To Ashok Vajpeyi,*
*a poet in search of heresy*

# CONTENTS

# INTRODUCTION
## In Praise of Heresy

History is one long struggle of heretics against orthodoxy and conformity. That is why social moments and individual instances of human freedom cannot be fully comprehended without paying some attention to the heretical actions that have emerged from within them. The role of heresy in the formation of critical thinking and anti-dogmatism is central, yet heresy is little understood by common people and even learned individuals. As such, not believing in a belief is often portrayed as more dangerous than the belief itself. Moreover, beliefs are most clearly and systematically articulated when they get created as forms of obedience or conformism.

Heresy, however, is the art of non-conformity, and for non-conformity, as Emerson says, 'the world whips you with its displeasure' (1903, 40). Nonetheless, every human is a heretic, a Prometheus stealing fire from the gods and giving it to humanity. It seems as if Olympus sent its insane heroes into our world to give us back our freedom. However, when heroes arrive among humans, they are not known as Olympians but as heretics. Of the works of heretics, history is the record. But history itself must be heretic, or it is nothing. In other words, there is properly no history, only heresy; for every mind must live history for itself. 'What it does not see, what it does not live, it will not know,' writes Emerson (1903, 6). And yet, human beings are complacent, conformist, and apologetic. They can no longer stand up and dare to say, 'I am a heretic,' therefore, 'I am' (*ego heretica ergo sum*).

As a result, our time is not the time of heretics. It is an age of conspiracy against the greatness and majesty of the soul. Thus, all concentrates: we are a mob and mobs do not think. But if we look wider, beyond every mob there is a heretic who refuses mediocrity and servility. As a matter of fact, rebelliousness is the only virtue to the heretic, who shines in every anecdote of humanity and has given the book of life its immense fame. It is perhaps because life is a heroic adventure to only those who do not take it for granted. As such, there has always been among heretics of history a heroic sense of freedom which declines servitude in any shape or any form. This has been neither an ideal nor a dream. It is the power to contemplate human freedom as a gateway to transcend the infancy and immaturity of humanity.

The problem is, in short, as Simone Weil puts it,

> [I]n spite of progress, man has not emerged from the servile condition in which he found himself when he was handed over weak and naked to all the blind forces that make up the universe; it is merely that the power which keeps him on his knees has been as it were transferred from inert matter to the human society of which he is a member. (1986, 173–4)

If we follow Weil with the idea that servitude is the natural condition of humankind, then heresy is a vital need of the human soul. This need is fully satisfied when individuals transcend their subjection to humiliation and falsehood. There is, therefore, a natural alliance between heresy and questioning. When one questions, he/she is no more a captive mind. A captive mind is a mind enclosed in platitudes and banalities which cannot dwell in truth. Weil expresses this as follows:

> A man whose mind feels that it is captive would prefer to blind himself to the fact. But if he hates falsehood, he will not do so; and in that case he will have to suffer a lot. He will beat his head against the wall until he faints. He will come to again and look with terror at the wall, until one day he begins afresh to beat his head against it; and once again he will faint. And so on endlessly and without hope. One day he will wake up on the other side of the wall. (1986, 89)

Being a heretic and standing on the other side of the wall does not always indicate that the element of empathy is missing in a person. Quite the contrary, heresy is an awareness of an element of common humanity against all forms of docility and tameness that create indifference and apathy. Actually, safeguarding of a person is only possible when the 'self' and the 'other' both act as heretics. The great misfortune of humanity is to have always searched for the balance between the 'self' and the 'other' in a balance of power. 'Once society is divided up into men who command and men who execute,' affirms Weil, 'the whole of social life is governed by the struggle for power' (1986, 163). However, the secret of the human condition is that there is no power without the interrelation of human actions. Man's greatness is, therefore, to be able to recreate his freedom through new actions. But this can only happen when nothing interposes itself between him and his freedom.

The notion of freedom is far from simple, and yet it is the first that has to be elucidated in order to approach heresy. Owing to the fact that there is never freedom but only the capacity to be free, heresy is simply to actualize the power of being free, which exceeds the very limited means that an individual has at his disposal. According to Spinoza, a thing is said to be free if it exists by the mere necessity of its own nature and is determined in its actions by itself alone. In other words, freedom is the ability to have options and to make choices, decisions, and value judgements. As such, for Spinoza, to be free is not only to be free from outward servitude but also from inward servility. As he puts it, 'It is the fact of obedience, not the motive for obedience, which makes a man a subject' (2009, 199).

If we turn to Emerson and Thoreau, we can see that self-trust is the essence of this inward freedom from servility. It is the state of a soul at war with conformism and petty celebrations of life which prevent one from achieving greatness. Inspired by the ancient Greeks and Romans, Hannah Arendt saw 'greatness' in the words and deeds of actors who through virtuousness and ethical existence constantly tried to surpass one another and achieve exemplary status. For Arendt, however, these virtuous actions depended on the existence of a communicative and nonconformist public sphere, whereas heretic actions, by definition, were not necessarily co-constitutive of the public sphere. What is important in a heretic mind is what Emerson calls a 'cathartic virtue'. Let us not forget that Aristotle describes 'catharsis' in his *Poetics* as the process of purification of emotions. He relates it to tragedy and to the sense of 'fear and pity' aroused by the tragic in the spectator. The essential tragic effect depends on how fear and pity can become allies. But we can interpret Aristotle's theory of 'catharsis' as a form of 'purification' or 'cleansing' of the mind. Catharsis is, thus, an ethical enlightenment and a self-formation (*Bildung*). As such, only a clear comprehension of what is involved in the struggle for inward and outward freedoms can bring about a state of critical mindedness.

If we trace the Greek roots of the word 'catharsis', we can say that the idea of 'purification' or 'cleansing' in the case of heretic thinking and action is far from the adjective *katharos*, which means 'pure' or 'clean'. On the contrary, it goes back to the idea of 'purge'. The heretic mind eradicates and expulses from its mental structure any non-critical thinking that lacks creativity and transformation. As Georg Simmel put it, 'The resistance which has to be eliminated is what gives our powers the possibility of proving themselves' (1971, 48). Thus, the characteristic of a genuine heretic is that he/she cannot be common and plain. On the contrary, there is something heroic about heresy, because it undergoes continual changes. As such, if a person can think heretically, he or she shall also see life heretically. This is the ultimate fact about heresy. A heretic mind is the captain of its own self-relying soul. Thus, with heresy, all is self-reliance. As Emerson says bluntly: 'Whoso would be a man must be a non-conformist' (cited in Herndon 1969, 90).

There is a time in every human being's life when he or she arrives at the conviction that instinctive action is not sufficient in the making of a heretic mind. However, because the soul is progressive, it can immerse itself in new principles. As a matter of fact, heresy is the activity which repairs the decays of the mind, whether wholly or partly. On the other part, excellence is a perpetual victory of the soul, celebrated not by cries of ambition and greed but by serenity and wisdom. This serenity, as a moment of nonconformity, announces the instant presence of greatness as a manner of the soul. It is this greatness that was celebrated by the Greeks and the Romans and inspired all through history the heretic mind with the broad design of renovating the principles of social life and political state of affairs. But let us not forget that even if the tendencies of the present times favour the ideas of complacency and conformism, we must not come to the conclusion that no single human being can defy and deny the authority of the laws and the values of our contemporary society. One way or another, the biggest foe of human civilization is not violence, but mediocrity that generates violence.

In its own way, heresy always was and always should be intolerant of mediocrity. And the blunter it is, the more intolerant it is of mass psychology. Heretic emancipation from the burden of history is also a revolution in human consciousness. As such, heresy is not a matter of belief but of doubt. The fact is that heresy is the primary condition of a plural society where freedom of thinking and creating can excite and encourage individuals to develop an aesthetic of criticality. This kind of aesthetic output, of course, could be considered as a genuine form of self-awareness that could dissipate illusions and lies. In short, the space within which the heretic mind operates is fulfilled with a range of potentialities, both creative and disruptive. The transcendent and transformative disruption of heresy rebels against all uniformity of the status quo. However, the essence of heresy consists also basically in a dissenting position against all varieties of monism and hegemonism.

If the basic job of the heretic is to serve truth—that is, to serve the creative aim of life—then it necessarily develops into a defence of a truthful life of questioning. Thus, the historical experience of heresy teaches us that any genuinely meaningful form of heretic thinking could disturb the apathetic peace of societies which, by excess of conformity, have lost the potential of living within the truth. Champions of truthfulness are hard to find, especially in an age of mediocrity and platitude. We belong to a time in which living in truth is in danger of being destroyed by the means of post-truth. Those who think beyond absolute truths cannot be followers and flatterers. As Nietzsche asserts, 'He who thinks much is not suited to be a party member: too soon, he thinks himself through and beyond the party' (2008, 18).

Thinking today is thinking dangerously. Actually, in today's climate of opinions, every effort of thinking is an act of dissent. Hence, the question is not whether thinking is or is not prejudicial to a thoughtless world. The question, for all those who cannot live without thinking and what it signifies, is merely to find out how, in a thoughtless world, the heretic act of thinking is possible. It is not enough to say in this regard that thinking is threatened by the incapacity of the masses to think. If that were true, the problem would be simple: an existential resentment of what Hannah Arendt called 'negative solidarity' (1958b, 315). But the problem is more complex, more serious too, since it has become apparent that the battle is waged within the process of thinking itself. The age of accelerated mediocrity and infantilism is so effective today only because it is kept alive not only by the masses but also by intellectuals themselves. If, faced with such a reality, we can preserve the subversive nature of thinking and if, conversely, faced with the world's mediocrity, we manage not to forget the immensity of the limitless sublime, then thinking will gradually recover its strength. To be sure, we must learn to handle ideas in a spirit of heresy, because, after all, thinking is a revolt against everything thought of and established in the world.

It is a fact that unthinking respect for truth is the greatest enemy of truth. Moreover, the great misfortune of the process of thinking in today's world is that it has lost its power of distancing itself from what is banal, superfluous, and mediocre. This reminds us of what Schopenhauer says: 'Power of discrimination, *esprit de discernement*, and consequently judgement: that is what is lacking' (1970, 224). But what Schopenhauer underlines as the lack of power of distinction is also a fear of thinking. We can trace this fear back to the fear of being called a 'heretic' and being rejected by the unholy crowds, as has been the case all through human history. But to be a heretic, to be sure, is to look at the world from an Olympian standpoint. As Schopenhauer puts it, 'Courage would consequently be a kind of endurance, and since it is endurance which gives us the capacity for self-denial and self-overcoming of any kind, courage too is, through it, at any rate related to virtue' (1970, 135). It is wonderful how often the individuality of every human being is related to his/her moral integrity and to the power of not being servile. As Spinoza says rightly, 'Everyone's right is defined by his power [*Unius cujusque jus potential ejus definitur*]' (2005, 31n1, 200). The question of individuality amounts, in the end, to whether anyone could have the right to make others conform to his/her own rules. If this question is answered affirmatively, then democracy has not come of age.

If democracy is powerless, then people's power is meaningless. This being so, it is not a surprise that democracies, despite their peaceful and law-abiding frameworks, have not been able to change the egoistic, greedy, and revengeful nature of human beings. This bitter reality encourages pessimistic, conservative, and anti-democratic thinkers such as Schopenhauer to believe that

> because the great majority of men are in the highest degree egoistic, unjust, inconsiderate, deceitful, sometimes even malicious, and equipped moreover with very mediocre intelligence, there exist the need for a completely unaccountable power, concentrated in one man and standing above even justice and the law, before which everything bows and which is regarded as a being of a higher order, a sovereign by the grace of God. Only thus can mankind in the long run be curbed and ruled. (1970, 152–3)

Schopenhauer's critical point on the incurable egoism of human crowds brings us to think of the heretical imperative as the only remedy to what appears as a permanent evil all through history. In truth, there is no necessary relationship between heresy and democracy. Though heretical minds can be autonomous catalysts in the shaping of democracies, we have to admit that neither electoral nor liberal democracies create heretical spirits.

A heretical spirit brushes everything aside because of his/ her acid reasoning and goes deep to the crucial and structural problem of democracies: mediocrity. If there is a gradual end to democracies in the contemporary world, it has certainly not been activated by a military coup or an authoritarian president, but by a steady erosion of democratic values and liberties. The tragedy of the situation is that at any street corner of the democracies in our time, the sentiment of mass mediocrity can strike any attentive and critical mind in the face. This mediocrity certainly runs through all the social media, political literature, and public discourses, and the everyday conformist and complacent citizens feed on them. One need only travel to Toronto and Dubai, the two extreme sides of the planet, to get a good feeling of how citizens, despite being in different cultures, actually absorb exactly the same amount of mediocre nonsense and untruth by watching their favorite Breakfast Television programmes. It is, therefore, essential and vital to know how we can remain intellectually immune from this mediocrity which hides behind the mask of excellence. So long as our minds remain heretically critical and doubtful of the things and events of the world, autonomy will be more readily expected from those who suggest and teach non-instrumental and non-calculative thinking.

If we look at the history of public intellectuals since Socrates up to the twenty-first century, we can recognize the quality of heretical excellence that was practised by very few in the battles against conformity and spiritual servility. For centuries, public intellectuals aligned themselves with this heretical imperative which was embodied by Socratic questioning and brought a complete change in the values of political and cultural life of humankind. In championing the shared space of questioning against or in parallel with organized power, heretic figures from the intellectual and artistic worlds opened up the domains of social, political, economic, and cultural life to public scrutiny and accountability. It was this heretic effort of questioning, a Socratic philosophical gesture of dissent, that exposed the flaws of authoritarian rule and the fallacies of justice from ancient

Athens to Ciceronian Rome and up to the modern times with
the philosophical movement known as the Enlightenment and,
finally, with the emergence of the figure of the 'intellectual' in
the Dreyfus Affair. Philosophers and artists with whose names
and works we are familiar—Michelangelo, da Vinci, Beethoven,
Mahler, La Boetie, Voltaire, Rousseau, Kant, Thoreau, Marx,
Zola, Sartre, Camus, Castoriadis, Chomsky, Said, and so on—
have questioned the nature of our thoughts and practices, and
have been inspirational and foundational to the invention and
disruption of laws, conventions, and institutions. That is why, the
public intervention of the creators of colours, words, concepts,
and values falls short of being dissenting and critical without
its heretical complement. Heretical thinking, therefore, has to
induct degrees of subversion and disruption. It is not a historical
accident that tyrants and dictators have always been afraid of
heretics and have at all times tried desparately to prevent them
from speaking and acting. But the truth is that heretics have
always pushed back against powers that seek to imprison bodies,
destroy thoughts, and stultify souls.

The importance of heretic thinking lies not so much in the
calculative and utilitarian essence of ideas but rather in why
and how these ideas bring changes to the history of humanity.
Apart from the contribution of heretics to the making of
history, the significance and importance of heresy has been
more than apparent in the process of strengthening, consoli-
dating, and defending creativity and the art of questioning. It
is worth remembering that one of the most fascinating periods
of heretical intervention in human history has been the period
of Enlightenment. The heretical thinkers of this period produced an enchanted world where emancipation and autonomy

became the key concepts of eighteenth-century Europe. As in the case of Socrates, the philosophical–political effort of the heretic *Aufklärers* (enlighteners) was translated by the freedom of examining, questioning, and criticizing. The struggle for the freedom of conscience, therefore, was accompanied by the critique of authority, both religious and political. The idea of the autonomy of reason was at the foundation of the principal idea that human beings were no more servants of God as they were no more subjects to kings. The two heretic ideas that shaped intellectual dissent in the eighteenth century were choice and doubt. The heretic imperative transformed human minds into free spirits and emancipated human societies from the tutelage of all forms of servitude. In other words, the exercise of the heretic mind in the eighteenth century results in the three ideas of respect for individual freedom, of the optimistic reading of history, and of the moral perfectibility of humanity.

Moreover, in eighteenth-century Europe, the quest for happiness replaced religious salvation. As for the denial of God as the foundation of modern politics, the new heretics of the eighteenth century ended by giving priority to respect for humanity instead of respect for God. Immanuel Kant, as the founder of German Idealism, defined the heretic essence of the Enlightenment as 'man's emergence from his self-incurred immaturity' (1991, 1). The immaturity that Kant was pointing at was encouraged, according to him, by laziness and cowardice. However, Kant developed clearly in his famous essay 'Beantwortung der Frage: Was ist Aufklärung?' (Answering the Question: What is Enlightenment?, 1784) the idea that human beings can grow up and grow away from their rulers and become independent. Kant's overall argument is that

Enlightenment is humankind's exit from a state of immature dependence. Kant's famous argument is that everyone should be able to enjoy equally and independently the freedom of public debate, which is 'the most innocuous form of all' (1991, 3). In Kant's view, we do not yet live in an 'enlightened' age but one which is in the process of becoming enlightened. Enlightenment, therefore, means making use of one's own understanding and judgment in the public space. The process of Enlightenment, however, requires that we emerge from what Kant calls *Unmündigkeit*, which means immaturity. Admittedly, Kant makes it clear that our only way to build a rational and free commonwealth is to attain intellectual maturity. Maturity, thus, is the capacity to determine autonomously one's own conduct. Heteronomy, by contrast, is interference with one's self-determination. As its Greek etymology denotes, the word heteronomy signifies the condition of an individual (or a group) who has lost its right to govern itself. Consequently, it presupposes that an individual remains in an infantile state of mind. On the contrary, autonomy, which is the central characteristic of a heretic mind, leads directly to social and political agency. According to Cornelius Castoriadis, 'One cannot want autonomy without wanting it for everyone and ... its realization cannot be conceived of in its full scope except as a collective enterprise' (1987, 107). This is mainly because the heretic mind has its beginnings not in the desire of self but within the otherness of the Other. Heresy has always to do with the Other. As such, if heresy as autonomy 'is the relation in which others are always present as the otherness and as the self-ness of the subjects, then autonomy can be conceived of, even in philosophical terms, only as a social problem and as a social relation' (Castoriadis 1987, 108). From this follows the question of self-creation. Where heteronomy limits the creativity of individuals and societies, heretical imperative creates self-reflectiveness and social autonomy.

Consequently, for a philosopher and enlightener such as Kant, undergoing the process of Enlightenment would lead human beings to become morally and rationally autonomous and participate in the creation of a communicative space of dialogue and peace. Undoubtedly, the intellectual interventions of the French, British, and German Enlightenments, in opposition to the social inequalities and moral mediocracies of the old hierarchical and religious order, represented great moments of the heretical revolution in eighteenth-century Europe. This new radical thinking about social autonomy and philosophical emancipation turned out to have immense heretical implications that few of its proponents, such as Voltaire, Rousseau, Diderot, and Kant, could certainly have anticipated. As in the examples of individuals such as Giordano Bruno (who confronted the authority of the Inquisition with his belief in many worlds and put into question the arguments of Copernicus and Kepler who mistakenly thought that the universe is spherical and the Sun is its centre), Étienne de La Boétie (a critic of modern authoritarian society), or Sir Thomas More (a martyr of conscience who believed in the primacy of truth over power), heretical thoughts and individual experiments with truth became the battle cries of those who created the vast stage of critical thinking for centuries to come.

Choosing to represent the powerless, heretical spirits became the outsiders in their worlds. They undermined the political structures of their times in their unfinished battle against mediocracy, orthodoxy, and populism. Kant asserted in his pamphlet on 'Perpetual Peace: A Philosophical Sketch' (1991, 37):

> As far as reason is concerned, the result is the same as if man's selfish tendencies were non-existent, so that man, even if he is not morally good in himself, is nevertheless compelled to be a good citizen. As hard as it may sound, the problem of setting up a state can be solved even by a nation of devils (so long as they possess understanding).

Kant's suggestion here is that the only way for a nation of devils to attain a good level of moral culture is to produce a good republican constitution. The exercise of freedom is, therefore, inscribed in the exigency and necessity of a universal republicanism which links the individual and communitarian enterprises of autonomy to the process of moral excellence.

But we live in a world which despises moral excellence as much as it is indifferent to individual autonomy. Maybe that is why in today's world, politics is no more a practice of morality but an art to lie. Thus, we are witnesses to a strange state of affairs: the idea of politics as a mode of organizing the society is no more subordinated to the ideas of conscience and responsibility, since it has become dependent on the choices of powerful companies and corporations. Maybe this is one of the reasons why education in contemporary societies is no more a democratic enterprise and a form of *paideia*, as the ancient Greeks called it, but a way of fabricating uncritical minds in search of diplomas and jobs. Nicolas de Condorcet, the famous French philosopher and mathematician of the eighteenth century, affirmed that the aim of education was 'to cultivate in each generation the physical, moral and intellectual faculties and thereby contribute to the general and gradual improvement of the human race' (cited in Simon 1972, 29). If education is not only about commonly shared values in a society but also about a constant emphasis on critical deliberation and moral judgement, then heresy is the safety valve of education as it is the last lifeboat of democracy in dark times.

A *paideic* state cannot be established only through laws and regulations. It needs both the never-ending heretical self-examination and moral responsibility. However, the idea that the world might actually be changed by the heretical spirit of truth with the interference of no lie, no corruption, and no violence is not new. All nations and cultures can go through a phase of Socratic self-awareness when and where they get involved in a struggle against their own civilizational nightmares and political hubris. For centuries, the basic component of critical minds has been metaphysical heresy which affirms intellectual responsibility against the evil of mediocrity and conformity. Those who dared to resist the thermodynamics of power and, to confront the dark side of history with the only heretical ethos at their disposal, took side not only with common sense and the power of reasoning against rubbish and nonsense but also with justice against injustice. This heretic act was not sheer protest, since a simple act of dissent, whether justified or unjustified, does not qualify one to be a member of the heretical circle of thinkers and creators. What does do so is a combination of belief in the power of questioning and the moral progress of humanity. And this, of course, has occurred much more in centuries where humanity had an acute sense of empathy, autonomy, and freedom than in today's world.

Heresy always goes hand in hand with a sense of independence. But what do we understand by independence in the twenty-first century? Oxford dictionary defines 'independence' as 'the fact or state of being independent' and characterizes 'independent' as 'free from outside control; not depending on another's authority'. In other words, when we are talking of 'independence' we are giving priority to what a person decides for himself/herself over what is imposed upon him/her from outside. Autonomy is, actually, the best word that designates this process of thinking by oneself and making one's own laws, norms, and rules without outside interference. In other words, the heretical struggle for one's independence is undoubtedly a fight for the freedom of conscience and for the moral dignity of individuals. The concept of responsibility is important here, because it shows up to what point the struggle for independence can enable individuals to enter political maturity. That is to say, the distinctive characteristic of the heretical spirit of independence is to have a capacity to improve oneself. Most probably nothing in the life of a human being is more important than the choice of maturity. This is a mode of thinking that enters in dialogue with what Cornelius Castoriadis calls an 'inherited thought' while subjecting it to a critical examination. According to Castoriadis, '[T]he object of philosophy is the question: What ought I, what ought we, to think—about being, about knowledge of Being, about "I", about "we", about our polity, about justice' (1991, 25). In this line of thought, a heretical thinking is a project of autonomy which can only exist if it questions its origins and its present and future activities. To be sure, when heretical thinking emerges it seeks its proper subject matter. But the implication here is that genuine heretical thinking always appears as a revolt, a rebellion, and a dissenting voice. Of course, the truth is that every act of questioning is an act of interrogating, doubting, and refuting. But the practice of doubting and questioning is not that of using violence or eliminating another idea or the person or nation that represents it. On the contrary, heretical thinking is the exercise of radical autonomous thinking against all modes of dogmatism and fanaticism, including blind and barbaric violence practised by an individual, a group, or a state. It is not because we are all born under the restraint of a past history and past traditions that we cannot have a reflective activity free of prejudice and violence. Actually, heretical thinking is a mode of questioning that deploys itself both autonomously and under the pressure of or in opposition to an authoritative past. With this observation in mind, we can say that it is actually the free exercise of the heretical spirit and the state of intellectual maturity that make philosophical questioning a process of doubting and a project of autonomy.

History cannot be rewritten as a function of the needs of the moment. Today's questions have become, in many respects, those of forgetting ends and sacralizing means. But what the heretical thinking asks of us is the so-called 'humanity as an end' formula. We should always act, according to Kant, in ways that recognize and affirm the humanity in ourselves and in our fellow human beings. Accordingly, heretical thinking considers individuals as inherently and objectively worthy human beings with a common dignity. It is recognizing the fact that everyone is due a measure of excellence and a commitment to cultivate the maturity of humanity. However, the true motivating force behind this commitment is not philanthropy but an empathetic and humanistic belief in the reflecting power of human beings to be individually and collectively autonomous. Therefore, truth is not a matter of architectonic systems of thought or monstrous ideologies. In the same manner, state power has no right to decide where the truth resides. As Voltaire said, 'When truth is evident, it is impossible for parties and factions to rise. There never has been a dispute as to whether there is daylight at noon' (cited in Saklofske, Reynolds, and Schwean 2013, 113). The fact is that a heretical dialogue around the idea of independence fosters a critical spirit, whereas a unifying discourse imposed by any authority tends to choke it. As Pascal says, 'A man does not show his greatness by being at one extremity, but rather by touching both at once' (1931, paragraph 353).

Immanuel Kant defines Enlightenment as humankind's release from its 'self-incurred tutelage'. It is the process by which human beings can become free of intellectual guardianship and learn to 'dare to think'. Kant believed that this tutelage occurred because of many reasons and aspects; cowardice and complacency being among them. In other words, for Kant, as for many of us, being mature is about being independent minded and morally and intellectually mature. This is where the force of heretical thinking resides: it helps individuals to think not only in terms of political autonomy but mainly in relation to intellectual and moral independence. Where there is a desire and a unity among citizens of a society to think for themselves and emerge from any form of tutelage, that society is already in its mode of questioning and on the path of its independence. This sense of maturity is at the heart of heretical thinking. Maturity is that which matters for heretical thinking. Moreover, the singularity of the heretical thinker emerges precisely from a mode of questioning. This mode of questioning is the only genuine self-examining that the singular heretical thinker can enact, provided that he/she takes part in its transformative becoming. As such, the heretical thinker who embraces this transformative becoming must also engage in the radical critique of all forms of heteronomy. Once again, to quote Castoriadis, 'Philosophy, creating self-reflecting subjectivity, is the project of breaking the closure at the level of thought' (1991, 20). We can add, thus, that there is a close relationship between nonconformist, non-complacent, and non-mediocre societies, and self-reflective citizens. A heretical society is, therefore, the by-product of heretical individuals. Heretical subjectivity is what allows self-reflective individuals to take a critical distance from their traditions, mores, and sociopolitical institutions. As a result, the task of thinking heretically cannot be undertaken as a simple act of pseudo-reading and pseudo-writing, where the thinker is not committed to or implicated in his/her heretical adventure. To be heretical is to ask: *Why and how we should think?* But there is another question: *What are we to think?* In other words, the challenge arising for the philosopher qua heretic is the challenge of thinking of heresy philosophically. That is to say, it is the thinking of heresy which affirms its possibility as a mode of thinking. But if thinking heretically is an integral part of the appraisal of heresy then it must be integral to the self-transformative capacity of heretical thinkers, creators, and practitioners. Thus, heretics should make a retreat in regard to the ambient mediocrity of the world. This is necessary precisely because the ontological possibility of the heretical imperative implicates an autonomous mode of thinking. This retreat becomes not only the place of dwelling of the heretical thinker but also a means to engage with the heretical imperative as the project of thinking.

In the present book, we take different philosophico-creative examples of such an engagement with the heretical imperative. Heresy is portrayed through the self-examined lives of philosophers such as Socrates and Ortega y Gasset, or the creative revolt of a writer-philosopher such as Albert Camus, or the aestheticization of death by a writer such as Yukio Mishima. These are all heretical temptations which elaborate the context of heretical imperative present in the central character of this research, B.R. Ambedkar. Nothing is nearer to truth than to affirm that Dr Ambedkar is the boldest heretic of Indian political history. Maybe that is why he was ignored by his contemporaries, and, to some extent, he continues to be ignored as a heretical thinker in our times. Some recognize his moral courage and political audacity, but he remains unread by many inside and outside India. He is misinterpreted by politicians and misread by philosophers. He has not entered the canon of modern Indian history. He remains among the apocrypha, an isolated figure to those who teach and learn modern Indian history in schools and universities. Though passionately admired by Dalits and a few Indian intellectuals, he is largely dismissed for his exit from Hinduism and his conversion to Buddhism. And yet, what Ambedkar shows us beyond the emancipative effort of the Untouchables and dissenting voices in today's India is that the promise of humanity is to move beyond itself. If conformity is the temperature of our times, Ambedkar is undoubtedly the anti-temperature. He is the heretical figure par excellence who speaks of reflective and critical thinking as a revolution. Here lies the sense of the unity of heresy and creativity. As Camus says, 'To create today is to create dangerously' (1995b, 251). For Ambedkar, to think dangerously is an ontological requirement. Here, the centrality of concern is to define the exemplarity of heretical imperative against the claims of totality. The experience of thinking as a heretic can be an extremely dangerous political act which does not have many allies. Of that we can be sure, but what Ambedkar, the heretical Indian, shows us is that, 'Freedom is not a gift received from a State or a leader but a possession to be won every day by the effort of each and the union of all' (Camus 1995a, 97).

A heretic lives only on the constraints he/she imposes on himself/herself. Grounded in the spontaneity of freedom, it is one of the clearest demands of rebellion. It is a rebellion against an unfinished meaning in the society. For Ambedkar, the true meaning of Indian society is one where caste is annihilated, but, more importantly, it is a historical moment of autonomous gathering. As such, Ambedkar's writings and speeches provide us a significant insight into Indian social, political, and cultural self-understanding. Further, the task which remains is to take seriously his position on democracy and on the nature of identity as well as on the revolution of values which can be given as a promise to the Indian society. It is to this effort, to grasp the philosophical and political resonances of Ambedkar's heretical thought as it echoes forth the waves of Indian society and beyond it our globalized world of prejudice, intolerance, and inequality, that this work is committed. We can take him at his words when he writes in reply to Mahatma Gandhi:

> The Hindus in the words of Mathew Arnold are 'wandering between two worlds, one dead the other powerless to be born'. What are they to do? The Mahatma to whom they appeal for guidance does not believe in thinking, and can therefore give

no guidance which can be said to stand the test of experience. The intellectual classes to whom the masses look for guidance are either too dishonest or too indifferent to educate them in the right direction. We are indeed witnesses to a great tragedy. In the face of this tragedy all one can do is to lament and say— such are thy leaders, O Hindus! (Rodrigues 2002, 318–19)

The major task which still remains to be done in our world is employing the heretical revolution as a frame of reference for intellectual criticism in the Indian society and beyond. Ambedkar's standpoint on the role of intellectuals is clear. Before turning to the body of the text, it may be helpful to focus briefly upon the scope and role of intellectuals as heretics.

Thinking about the heretical role of intellectuals in today's world, and more specifically in India, is of great significance, given the changes taking place in culture and politics. It is not enough to simply talk about the role of Indian intellectuals in the making and preserving of critical mindedness and democratic engagement in Indian academia. One should also pay attention to the role which could and should be played by public intellectuals in promoting moral and political excellence and civic friendship among the future generation of Indians. However, to do so, intellectuals in India need to challenge the traditional assumptions that have reinforced positivistic methodologies, apathetic scholarship, and an increasing fascination with a calculative leadership which refuses to listen and to learn instead of leading. Yet, we should not forget that the notion of critical thinking and the business of questioning, more than being acts of political partisanship, are essential components of the definition of 'intellectual' in modern times. The twenty-first century represents in general a separation between intellectuals and the public space. Seldom have intellectuals and the political world diverged so much. As such, intellectuals are no more described as 'superheroes of the mind' but simply as critical idealists who look beyond the scope of our everyday life. Today, heretical intellectuals are an endangered species. But most intellectuals have a fear of the political, and it seems as if the political has also a terrible indifference to what could be called 'intellectual'. Many others have seen this process as a decline of the intellectual. This decline is usually described as a process of distancing from the public sphere toward an increasingly professionalized, corporate, and managerial world. In other words, intellectuals are losing their public authority and their moral legitimacy of speaking truth to power, while becoming incapable of carrying on their independent and critical functions as thinkers and animators of ideas. The move of the intellectuals away from the public sphere can be described as an effort to renegotiate the purpose and boundaries of the public sphere without taking into consideration the ethical imperatives of a dialogue with the political. Therefore, today's intellectuals seem to think that since all moral truths are relative, there is no more a need to represent a moral voice in a voiceless world. The attempts of the intellectuals in the academia and other professional institutions to pretend that it is politically correct and wise to be dismissive of moral imperatives in the public sphere is a way of coinciding the humanitarian urge of our world with the special needs of career-making. Salaried, tenured, and pensioned, many intellectuals find themselves chained to the wheel of a respectable career and profession, which grounds their capacity of critical mindedness in a non-adversarial context. More precisely, narrow professional self-interests have destroyed the so-called public interests of the intellectuals. Quickly and unrepentantly forgetting their moral and political responsibilities, many intellectuals in today's world have degraded and abandoned the idea of the public sphere, evolving into uncritical supporters of mass culture. It is by virtue of this uncritical public stance that political and cultural experts and media pundits have replaced intellectuals as the sociological actors of our contemporary world. Engaged solely in discussing facts—that is, facts dictated by the economic laws of the market or by the political decisions of governments around the world—today's media celebrities are no more interested in discussing values.

With the rise of the post-industrial global village, dominated by media networks and technology-led communication in which critical voices are often drowned, what can be called the 'epidemic of conformism' has completely paralysed and rendered impotent the critical questioning of the intellectuals. That said, the category of 'intellectual' remains a problematic concept and difficult to define. However, in order to question the role of intellectual engagement in the context of the twenty-first century, we need to start with some of the salient features of the intellectual in history. It goes without saying that the intellectual has always been a social-historical figure that has emerged from a cultural background but with a public function that relates to a universal consciousness. This emphasis on the universal task of the intellectual and its presence as a sociopolitical figure in the public space reinforces the distinction between 'intellectuals' and 'academics'. Moreover, with 'intellectuals' the focus is not only on the transmission of ideas but also on the act of universalizing awareness through a process of questioning. In other words, the critical mode of questioning which is proper to the work of intellectuals is an engagement with the problem of questioning itself and not only with the capacity to question and to doubt. So, perhaps the basic question of intellectual questioning is about the meaning, validity, and legitimacy of questions.

Therefore, by definition, society for an intellectual is a space of active questioning and unlimited interrogation in such a way that the questions of freedom, justice, equity, and equality can always be posed anew and not taken for granted. It doesn't come to us as a surprise that the history of political thought began with an act of intellectual questioning, that of Socrates, the Athenian philosopher and gadfly, against his judges who condemned him to death. If Socrates can be considered as the first public intellectual in the history of humanity, it is certainly because he is something other than a simple Athenian picked out of the crowd. He is an individual who took his distance from his own heritage by questioning the nature of Greek myths and ideas. Socrates's main accomplishment is to call into question the conventional forms of authority and heteronomy of his time. Thus, Socrates is not only a philosopher-citizen but also a philosopher-heretic. This idea of 'heresy' is a key feature of the existential presence and the epistemological attitude of the intellectual in all times. Though the term 'intellectual', as we know it today, has been fabricated very late in human history, the critical function of intellectual thinking and the dissenting attitude of those who go against the tide has always been the mode of being for disobedient minds all through history.

It is with the Dreyfus Affair in nineteenth-century France (when Alfred Dreyfus was imprisoned in 1894 on charges of leaking secrets to the German army) that the category of the 'intellectual' became recognized for the first time, accompanied by a slightly different interpretation of its 'public' role. Despite the ideological differences among intellectuals during the Dreyfus Affair, both sides agreed that the intellectual should be engaged. But what an intellectual such as Emile Zola saw at stake in the Dreyfus Affair was to be able to use his ideas as a way to denounce injustice. Zola's pamphlet, *J'accuse*, became the critical spear of many writers, artists, journalists, and academicians who jointly signed a 'manifesto' and declared Dreyfus innocent and wrongly imprisoned.

Let us point out clearly that intellectuals are not only individual thinkers but also public servants of humanity who stand for something far larger than the discipline from which they originated. They are constantly balancing the private and the public. That is to say, an intellectual's personal commitment to an ideal must have relevance and respect for the society. This is how the intellectual engages himself or herself with the changing issues of society while remaining true to certain ethical principles. This is how intellectuals appear as the moral conscience of their societies. One of the tasks of the intellectual is to think. But can we think without disobeying, without questioning, and without dissenting? 'The most thought-provoking thing about our thought-provoking age,' wrote Martin Heidegger, is 'that we are still not thinking' (Heidegger 1976, 6). Thinking, Heidegger observes, is questioning. To think is to put the world and ourselves into question. In other words, thinking is determined by a person who questions. It involves not only our receptivity to freedom but also the necessity to disobey. The call of thought is, thus, the call to freedom. There has been, since Socrates, the tradition of a public intellectual as the supporter and guardian of civic freedoms. Let us ask what should public intellectuals stand for and fight for in today's world. Passive intellectualism and intellectual elitism are both precisely what intellectuals cannot afford at a time when they are trying to bring together a global community of shared values in order to confront global challenges all together. However, it happens that the specialization of intellectual life together with the dominance of mass culture has caused the disappearance of the charismatic public intellectual figure and the decline in the quality of what we call 'public'.

Today, intellectuals play no more the role of a critical counter power to liberal oligarchies and populist regimes around the world, and have lost their ability to think independently without being the actors of 'celebrity culture'. With the banalization of cultural life, intellectuals have been transformed into insignificant figures who find their homes in universities and think tanks around the world, where they have no moral legitimacy in their specific disciplines. This is an age of 'Trumpization of politics', an age of ignorance, arrogance, and mediocrity. This is an age which has brought with it the rise of populist politicians and loudmouth demagogues around the world. However, the rise of the demagogues is a symptom, not the cause, of the erosion of public trust and engagement. But what is often lost in the debate is the role that needs to be played by heretical intellectuals as agents to transform the public discourse and lead the society towards new social imaginaries and modes of thinking. It is time, once again, for heretical intellectuals to be the uncompromising fighters on behalf of human dignity.

# I
## AGAINST THE TIDE

# I

## THINKING AS HERETICS
### A Self-Examined Life

'Revolution is the mother of philosophy,' wrote Ambedkar in
*Philosophy of Hinduism* (cited in Ambedkar 1987, volume 3, 8).
In the same line of thought, one can add that heresy is the power
of thinking. Heresy, that is to say the potential of stepping out of
the framework or going against the current, is also the capacity
to hold something just as being true. The significance of thinking
in the world and about the world constitutes the value of heresy.
Thus, the best in the sense of the nobility of human spirit is
the capacity of heretic questioning. The unique paradox of this
situation is such that, even though the progress of civilization
has always been the work of heretics, civilizations are themselves
the destroyers of heretics. Thus, those who contemplated the
future of mankind from heretical perspectives, were all, during the past centuries, inspired by a sense of danger. They lived
with a rare conviction that everything had become question-
able and that history was no more inspired by a consciousness
of its nullity. As compared with these heretics, we have become
meaningless creatures for whom the awareness of life has ceased

to exist. That is why we live in a process of changing life which enforces no change in our mode of thinking. It follows, then, that humankind is voyaging upon an uncharted sea, unable to reach any shore which will give it a clear perspective on the whole.

We are living through the most meaningless century in the history of humankind and this meaninglessness has produced a sentiment of false peace which accompanies all our conformist wishes and complacent actions. However, Man without a sense of revolt would have no moral being. There are no more moments of revolt in the lives of human beings and nations afflicted by vanity. As Pascal says,

> Anyone who does not see the vanity of the world is very vain himself. So who does not see it, apart from young people whose lives are all noise, diversions, and thoughts for the future? But take away their diversion and you will see them bored to extinction. Then they feel their nullity without recognizing it, for nothing could be more wretched than to be intolerably depressed as soon as one is reduced to introspection with no means of diversion. (2013, 73)

What Pascal is referring to is the etymological sense of the word 'vanity' derived from the Latin *vanitas*, which means void and vacuum. Man is miserable, says Pascal, because vanity is inscribed in the heart of Man. As a result, humanity is unsteady and fluctuating with a fragile existence. It needs self-esteem and self-awareness beyond its hateful self. For Pascal, self-knowledge entails a change in self-love and, in the long run, in the whole human subjectivity. Nearly a 100 years before Pascal, Montaigne considered self-knowledge as the beginning of all wisdom. This heretical assertion, imperative in the form, indicates that mankind must stand and look at itself.

The heretic revolution initiated by Socrates had its starting point in the motto 'know thyself' inscribed on the front of the Temple of Delphi. The heretical imperative in the formula 'know thyself' invites mankind to look at itself. This defining of the self as, at some point, conscious of itself appears acutely in Camus's definition of the intellectual as someone 'whose mind watches itself' (1963, cited in Zaretsky 2011, 27). Heretics have always been characters who have been both the watchers and the watched. For the heretic who watches the world and the self, the 'watcher' eventually vanishes into the act of 'watching' itself. Maurice Merleau-Ponty wrote over 60 years ago, 'true philosophy consists in relearning to look at the world' (1962 [1945], xxiii). This is a task that philosophical thinking has been doing since Socrates and his heretical revolution. Perhaps calling Socrates the first heretic of history will come to many as a surprise, not to say a blasphemy. But what is the subject matter of philosophy if not 'questioning' and the 'questioning of questions'? And how can we characterize the history of heretical thinking if not as a perpetual effort to formulate questions? Yet, after 26 centuries of questioning, the scope of heretical thinking does not seem greatly diminished by this process of questioning. Heresy fed on the intellectual needs, social interests, political fears, and philosophical hopes of all heretics who thought against the trend and swam against the current. Socrates was the first to draw the crucial distinction between the conformist crowds and the dissenting individuals. Socrates had first-hand experience of the crowds of Athens. In 399 BCE, the philosopher was charged with corrupting the youth of Athens and was put on trial. A jury of 500 Athenians decided that Socrates was guilty. He was put to death by hemlock in a process which has remained as the first act of burning a heretic at the stake.

Socrates initiated the perennial task of heretics, which is to operate in the open and ask radical and non-conforming questions about the world and human existence. The figure of Socrates and his mode of living and thinking have largely contributed in the past 25 centuries to inspiring generations of heretics. The heretical thinking of Socrates, therefore, results in what he called 'the examined life'. Socrates combined the *daimonion*, his inner voice that provided him with a safeguard against all forms of dogmatism and fanaticism, with the pursuit of heretical wisdom. After all, because of the emphasis Socrates placed on the courage of thinking against the current, his philosophy helped generations of heretics give shape to their dissent in a manner that enabled what the likes of Reverend Martin Luther King, Jr, called 'a revolution of values' (1967, 33) centuries later. What King was specifying here is very much the same as Socrates's idea of 'self-examination'. For Socrates, 'an examined life' was a life of autonomy, where individuals became capable of self-instituting their destiny. This is why Socrates thought that philosophy as a form of knowledge is a 'lordly thing' which cannot be 'dragged about as if it were a slave' (cited in Vlastos 1995, 44). To confirm his belief in philosophy as an examined life and a self-knowledge, Socrates fostered tolerance for the points of view of others and offered time and space for discussion and dialogue. In the same manner, for Dr King, self-examination was not simply a way to self-institute one's destiny but a moral force that could bring about a revolution of values and a social self-transformation. From this he derived what he later called 'a revolution of values' in the American society and in the world. Dr King and Socrates both believed that values have power and that they are not 'words, words, mere words', as William Shakespeare writes in *Troilus and Cressida* (1602). But this has been the story of all heretics throughout human history, who believed that an 'examined life' and a 'revolution of values' better suited their moral temperaments and philosophical concerns. Among the thinkers of the twentieth century, José Ortega y Gasset is the one philosopher who is exposed more than others to this heretic sensibility of letting his better self be in control of his destiny.

Albert Camus said of Ortega y Gasset that 'after Nietzsche, [he] is perhaps the greatest "European" writer, and yet it would be difficult to be more Spanish' (cited in Landauer 1989, 272). By this, Camus meant that though Ortega is a typical Spanish thinker, his writings and his mode of thinking range far beyond the local concerns of the Iberian Peninsula. Camus and Ortega never met, but their philosophies represent an alarming view of the danger of retrogression of European culture and Western civilization in general to a state of barbarism and mass conformity, in sharp contrast with the naïve liberal faith in the idea of progress. For both Camus and Ortega as heretics, the idea of the inevitability of progress ultimately leads to disaster and obscurantism. For both Camus and Ortega, there is no historical necessity for progress toward a better state. Future is only possible through the knowledge of the past. Therefore, the quest for liberty is impossible without a quest for excellence, which is the result of human capacity to mold the institutions of its own choosing. As such, the 'truth of destiny' of a self-examined polity depends upon the nobility of spirit of the gadflies, not the complacency of the masses. In considering Ortega's treatment of this problem, it is more convenient to consider separately three dimensions of his general argument on the perversion of democracy and the rise of plebeianism. First is his characterization of democracy as a 'noble idea' under the shadow of which 'has sprouted in the public conscience a perverse preference for everything low' (1957, 53); second is his discussion of what he calls 'the lowering of the standards of civility' (cited in Bonefeld 2017, 56); and the third is his Socratic attempt to call his contemporaries to the examined life and to engage them in the activity of philosophizing.

Ortega's central question is how humankind can give meaning to its life, not as a state of being but as a task where history is realized as self-fabrication. For Ortega, this programme of life is not a progress towards a definitive aim transcending history, which would imply the arresting of the creativeness of human thought. On the contrary, for Ortega, thinking has a significant role in the vital process that unites all living things at all times. As such, according to Ortega, setting any standards other than life itself could cut the human culture from its vital impulse and lead to extreme rationalism and utopianism. As such, if historical truth and not biological utility constitutes reality, each effort of self-examination for every individual, nation, and especially each generation becomes a contribution to the whole scheme of life. Therefore, the great task confronting the contemporary world is to overcome the duality of the rational and the vital, so that universal history displays the inexhaustible capacity of human beings in succeeding to create countless things that nature could never produce by itself. As a result, he declared that reason should be interdependent with and subordinate to life. By making human life his focal point, Ortega emphasizes on the fundamental reality of inter-individual relations marked by reciprocity and mutual responsibility. This encounter of the individual with the Other is differentiated from what society is, which according to him is idolized by modern thought. As he says in his book *Man and People*:

> The collective soul, *Volksgeist* or 'national spirit', social consciousness, has had the loftiest and most marvelous qualities attributed to it, sometimes even divine qualities. ... And here our analysis with no special effort or premeditation, with no formal precedents (at least so far as I am aware) among philosophers, drops into our hand something disquieting and even terrible—namely, the collectivity is indeed something human, but the human without man, the human without spirit, the human without soul, the human dehumanized. (1963a, 174–5)

This dehumanized human is the plebeian who denies the dimension of the personal in his life. According to Ortega, this is how the dehumanized human espouses nihilism without choosing among the possibilities that define his/her destiny. This relapse into barbarism of the dehumanized human is the clear expression of Ortega's distrust of the contemporary form of society. This view of society accounts for Ortega's echoing of his fear of the rule of average standards through the masses. Beyond this, Ortega's political perspective concerns a balance between the individual and the community with an estimate of individual worth and creative democracy. Ortega's condemnation of the masses, therefore, goes hand in hand with what he calls the 'degeneration of the heart' and 'the wounding of the very principle which gave rise to democracy' (from 'Democracia Morbosa', cited in Westler and Craiutu

2015, 590). He affirms, 'Democracy as democracy—that is, strictly and exclusively as a standard of political equity— seems an admirable thing. But over-stimulated democracy, exasperated democracy, democracy in religion or art, for instance, democracy in thought and gesture, democracy of the heart and custom, is the most dangerous affliction which a society can contract' (Ortega and Kerrigan 1957, 54). This whole crisis of democracy, according to Ortega, is related to the exhaustion of humankind's vital possibilities. It is in the spirit of this idea of crisis that the heretical standpoint of Ortega y Gasset finds all its pertinence and relevance. The task that he set for himself as a philosopher was to address the problem of a crisis of the European mind in particular and of Western civilization in general.

For Ortega, the solution to the problem of our age hinged upon whether philosophy can create and illuminate the distinction between mere opinion (*doxa*) and true knowledge (*episteme*), between how the world is and what it ought to be. Philosophy, for Ortega, had a role of educating democracy. The rise of thoughtless individuals, he suggested, led to the advent of the new barbarian and the eclipse of culture. Hence, Ortega cherished thinking, which included for him questioning life in general. Ortega described civilization in *The Revolt of the Masses*, as 'the will to live in common'. Therefore, according to him, 'A man is uncivilized, barbarian in the degree in which he does not take others into account' (1932, 76). The process of not thinking and not listening to the other reached its height precisely in the mass-man. Against this state of thoughtlessness and what he called 'spiritual barbarism', Ortega suggested the idea of living and thinking.

Much of Ortega's work can be understood as a response to the rise of masses and the decline of thinking. That is why he described contemporary culture as 'the spoiled child of human history' who 'does not represent a new civilization struggling with a previous one, but a mere negation' (Ortega 1932, 98, 190). There are many different ways of understanding what Ortega meant by the decline of thinking, but to my mind his main concern was to get individuals to value philosophy and practise it for themselves. 'Thinking is a dialogue with circumstances,' wrote Ortega in 1942 in his *Notes on Thinking* (cited in Rogers 1994, 503). In other words, he sought like Socrates to engage his contemporaries in the activity of philosophizing and questioning and called them to the examined life.

In Chapter 14 of his book, *The Revolt of the Masses*, Ortega y Gasset describes Socrates as 'the great townsman, quintessence of the spirit of the polis' (1932, 152). By this he means that being 'Socratic' is philosophizing openly in the public space. Practically and tangibly connecting philosophy and politics in every regime is a risky matter. Death is the price that Socrates paid in order to make politics accountable to philosophy. For Ortega, the Socratic heretic, philosophy was his life, and his life was his practice of philosophy. For him, Socrates marked a decisive moment in the history of heretical thinking, in his effort to give a new and solid meaning to the idea of questioning in life. Ortega's heretical commitment as an outsider, but also as a questioning philosopher in public space, appeals only to those who continue to believe in the heretical imperative of dissenting through questions. The merest glance at his writings and intellectual engagements reveals that he remains a Socratic intellectual with an ideal of human excellence as an antidote to nihilism. Man, said Ortega, is a living creature born in a circumstance. At every moment, we need to be aware of our historical roots and our civilizational heritage. But he is warning of the possibility of civilization simply evaporating as a result of the fact that 'the directing of society has been taken over by a type of man who is not interested in the principle of civilization' (Ortega 2006, 195). To this, he adds: 'The world is a civilized one: its inhabitant is not: he does not see the civilization of the world around him, but he uses it as if it were a natural force' (2006, 196). The crucial question he poses here is that of responsible thinking and acting in a meaningless world. Philosophizing for him is, thus, not only a question of creating concepts but a wider heretic resistance against the loss of meaning of freedom as autonomy. He offers a way of thinking about freedom that renews the Socratic rebellious ethos of the heretic in the public space. The exemplary feature of this heretic ethos of rebellion is devoted to a courageous attempt to rescue the individual from the multiple manifestations of injustice and suffering in history. Therefore, the activity of thinking for him is not only a question of reasoning but the most transformative form of questioning. To this end, he recognizes the Socratic ethics of interrogation as an explicit political imperative exercised in the midst of a situation of uncertainty and ambiguity.

All through his life, as a heretic, Ortega refused to confine his thoughts within the rigid framework of a system. As such, his 'metaphysics of life' remained a philosophy of dialogue and diversity. His horror of the shallow conventional Spanish traditionalism not only made him substitute his thoughtful Europeanism for Hispanicism but also made him stand out as

a heretical thinker against the traditional academic philosophy. What he preached constantly in his philosophical career
and consistently carried on against wind and tide was the affir-
mation of philosophy as self-affirmation. Therefore, according
to Ortega, 'To live is to be outside oneself, to realize oneself'
(1956, 131). For him, life is the foundation which needs to
be made, to be realized, and to be lived. Self-realization is
the ultimate goal. Thus, his philosophy is designed to treat
culture as a path to self-realization. Moreover, in his eyes, 'All
the work of culture is interpretation—clarification, explana-
tion, or exegesis—of life' (1963b, 98). Culture is the moment
of clarity and security in the midst of chaos. In the same way,
philosophy and art are for Ortega forms of self-creation and
self-reflection. In his opinion, open-mindedness suits the cultivated spirit and encourages creativity. He, therefore, rejects
the narrow-minded view that there is only 'one way of seeing'
reality. Here lies his continuous effort to take philosophy
not for granted but as a heretical task that we must account
for unceasingly. Long before it was fashionable to do so, he
decided not to rest in some type of 'existential philosophy'
but to get engaged in a heretical thought concerned with
understanding all things in terms of a dialogue with the world.
In his 'Commentary on Plato's Banquet' (1946), he wrote:
'The world is toward us and we are towards the world'. Here
'the mutual and reciprocal existing of man and the world' was
brought into view by his 'heretical philosophy' as 'a permanent and constitutive state of mind' (cited in Rogers 2003, 61;
and Dobson 2009, 165).

Camus would certainly agree with Ortega that humanity had
no recourse but to continue thinking heretically, for it would

always discover that it has not thought anything out completely. Lastly, Camus, like Ortega (or Socrates for that matter), would insist that the first principle of a philosophy is the justification of itself, a task that neither Ortega nor Camus forgot in his dissenting vision as a public heretic.

# 2

# HERESY AND REBELLION
Confronting Tyranny and Mediocrity

At no other time, perhaps, has the attack on thinking been deeper and more effective than in ours. Since Gautama Buddha, who, by approaching the concept of faith not as something external but as an awareness of the depth of one's own being, made a great heretic shift in the Hindu thought, up to Babasaheb Ambedkar, who stood against the dehumanizing sociopolitical structures of the Hindu social system, the significant and dissenting forms of heresy have followed one another. A whole family of heretical minds around the globe and through centuries have struggled in fighting against the consolidation and normalization of truth, suggesting new modes and paths of approach to understanding the human race. As such, all through the ages, heretical minds continuously strived to show that another mode of thinking and another way of living are possible. They knew which lies to fight and how to speak truth to power. Interestingly, a great number of the heretics of human history did not remain silent in confronting religious orthodoxies or philosophical dogmas. Some even put their lives at stake reforming systems of thought or fighting against tyrannies. Heretics of history were great minds who by fighting tyrannies and raising individuals from vassalage and lethargy helped them emerge from their self-incurred infantilism.

It is time for critical spirits to look for the substance of their intellectual independence by seeking a new relationship with the metaphysics of heresy. Undoubtedly, this return to heresy is the true task today. This metaphysical exercise of heresy is, of course, possible only when we understand, in the philosophical sense, that we need to transcend the horizon of our selfish interests and become involved with the moral imperatives that support our dissidence. Actually, if heresy is a perfect example of undogmatic thinking and dissent, then being a heretic is to break the silence and stand out as a disturber and an irritant in this era of complacency and widespread conformism. To paraphrase Vaclav Havel (1990, 167), a heretic cannot fit into any role that might be assigned to him, nor can he ever be made to fit any of the histories written by the victors. As it was pointed previously, a heretic is an outsider and a stranger. He or she doubts systems, either philosophical or political. For this very reason, a heretic is at rebellion against all forms of mediocre truth and existential ignorance. Paradoxically, the heretic finds compensation and inspiration in every disappointment. Heretics' best hopes come after their greatest disappointments because, as Friedrich Schiller says, 'disappointments are to the soul what a thunderstorm is to the air' (cited in Balachandran 2009, 36). As a thunderstorm freshens up the air, heretical disappointments smarten up the mind. As such, life for a heretic should be a school of patience and humility. This means that what is essential is not only to live heretically but learning to live heretically.

This is a difficult task, though heresy is an essential dimension of humanity. We should understand that heresy is not the most fairly distributed thing in the world.

Living heretically is, actually, giving value to life, but also understanding that life is not valuable if it is not approached heretically. As Montaigne, one of the most significant philosophers and writers of the French Renaissance, said: 'Life is a tender thing, and easily molested' (1870, 558). If the heretic is on the side of life and truth and knows how to live in truth without possessing it, then he/she is always at odds with the victors, whoever they may be and wherever they practise their authority. Living in truth means to be on neither side of the story. But it also means having the power of disobeying authority and undermining tyrannies. Unlike crowds who learn to live with lies and spend time with them and in them, heretics do not confirm and fulfill the system. To use Havel's words, to live within truth is to be able 'to find an outlet for [one's] creativity' (1985, 51). There is an ethical dimension to Havel's concept of creativity which echoes Camus's dimension of artistic and intellectual creations.

Camus's work has a considerable value for the culture of heresy. He was deeply involved, both in deeds and words, in some of the major heretical battles of his time. As he underlines in his Nobel Prize acceptance speech in December 1957: 'Probably every generation sees itself as charged with remaking the world. Mine, however, knows that it will not remake the world. But its task is perhaps even greater, for it consists in keeping the world from destroying itself' (Camus 1958, 34). His perspective of creativity goes hand in hand with his politics of rebellion, which form the ontological and ethical conditions of heretical intervention in the world. However, his belief is that the logic of rebellion should leave no space for murder. In the same manner, we can say that the act of heresy does not open any space for violence. Since heresy places a positive value upon life, it is the initial experience of the individual who believes in rejecting and criticizing the act of violence. This critique and negation of violence translates into an identification of the heretical imperative with the universality of humanity.

> For Camus, rebellion means not only an individual and collective refusal of death and absurdity in the name of nature and happiness; it comes to imply resistance to physical or political oppression as well—for such oppression is on the side of death and misery in negating men's freedom and happiness. Camus' basic intent at this point is to establish that there are intrinsic limits to the kind of treatment which may be meted out to human beings, if their essential humanity is to be preserved. (Willhoite, Jr 1961, 404)

Camus suggests that the question of rebellion is the problem of freedom, and as a result only an individual well aware of his/her freedom has the requirements to be rebellious. That is why, as Camus adds, rebellion is 'humanity's gradual self-awareness' (1956, 20). This awareness is the basis of solidarity among human beings, which can justify rebellion. If we walk in Camus's shoes, we can add that since heresy is a form of rebellion, heresy and human solidarity are intimately related. There is no need, however, for extended comments upon this relationship, since all human beings agree that there is evil and injustice in the world. As Schopenhauer puts it: 'There is not much to be got anywhere in the world. It is filled with misery and pain; if a man escapes these, boredom lies in wait for him at every corner. Nay more; it is evil which generally has the upper hand, and folly that makes the most noise. Fate is cruel and mankind pitiable' (2012, 18). The only value for Camus is morality, but a morality that is not rooted in God but in a compassionate vision of justice. That is to say, all heretical protest against the conditions of human existence is a cry for justice in the face of injustice. Heresy, therefore, allows for compassion and empathy insofar as its first steps are taken towards a solidarity among men in which suffering loses its sting. It is perhaps because heresy is not the way of the gods but that of human beings. Here, thus, is an attempt at a human-made protest which could be identified with the history of heresy. Though it is true that history sets some limits on heretical action, it is also true that heretics set some limits upon history, and that comes with the critique of violence.

Is violence wrong? This is a crucial existential question. In answering this question, Camus distinguishes between humane revolt and murder in the name of an ideal. For Camus, no ideal can justify murder. Unlike Mahatma Gandhi and Martin Luther King, Jr, Camus does not advocate pure non-violence, but he attempts to demonstrate that the refusal to kill or to legitimize murder is the starting point for living together. 'For my part,' he writes in his powerful pamphlet *Ni victimes ni bourreaux* (*Neither Victims nor Executioners*), 'I am fairly sure that I have made the choice. And, having chosen, I think that I must speak out, that I must state that I will never again be one of those, whoever they be, who compromise with murder, and I must take the consequences of such a decision' (2008, 53). Here, Camus invites us to reflect on the problem of heresy as an ethical protest and a moral revolt against violence. He calls for a move away from abstract principles in favour of the value of human dignity.

As in the case of his play *Les Justes* (1949) in this essay Camus is concerned with the effects of murder, terrorism, and other forms of violence on the perpetrators, and not only on their victims. For him, the revolution is not a valid justification to kill and eventually destroys ethical beliefs. As such, confronted with all the evils of the world, Camus reveals a philosophical deadlock, since for him violence is both unavoidable and unjustifiable. But if we go back to Camus's critique of revolution, we can understand why he accuses revolutionaries of not tolerating rebels and demanding them to accept conformity. In the same vein, we can say that revolutions are, by essence, anti-heretical and in all cases request heretics to conform to the limits of history as rewritten by the revolutionaries. As a matter of fact, the spirit of revolution wrongly considers heresy as merely an object of historical necessity. However, such a distortion is unacceptable to the logic of creativity. If we understand creativity as a heretical presence in history, then the aesthetics of banality pushed forward violently by the so-called historical necessity of revolutions is the distortion of creativity itself. Creativity, thus, is a breakaway from necessity, either aesthetic, political, or historical. Moreover, according to Camus, 'Art leads us back to the origins of rebellion, to the extent that it tries to give its form to an elusive value which the future perpetually promises, but of which the artist has a presentiment and wishes to snatch from the grasp of history' (1956, 227). In other words, the real significance of heresy is the centrality of creativity as a trans-historical dimension. Here is where the common value of humanity is maintained. Consequently, the heretic should perpetuate with renewed seriousness the very existence of creativity in the face of evil. Therefore, the only rule of moral conduct would be the recognition of the positive value of creative freedom. As such, the logic of creativity is itself the logic of heresy as the most exemplary expression of social and political freedom.

Heresy, as it is described here, is the universal a priori of human community, which is founded on the value of remaining faithful to the world. This is to say, heresy is confronting the meaninglessness and thoughtlessness of life and the absurdity of death. From such a perspective, the life of a heretic thinker and creator is that of, what Camus calls, 'celebrated culpability'. Culpability generally requires choice (*hairesis*: αἵρεσις), the possibility of choosing an action over its alternatives. And the act of choosing brings responsibility. It is this question that occupied Hannah Arendt through most of her life and laid the foundation of her call to critical thinking as a solution to the problem. What makes Arendt's heretic stand also interesting is her reference to the ethic of worldliness accompanied by an agonistic conception of interconnectedness, which would enable citizens to assume political responsibility. As Arendt affirms in her opus magnum, *The Human Condition*:

> Action, the only activity that goes on directly between men without the intermediary of things or matter, corresponds to the human condition of plurality, to the fact that men, not Man, live on the earth and inhabit the world. ... Plurality is the condition of human action because we are all the same, that is, human, in such a way that nobody is ever the same as anyone else who ever lived, lives, or will live. (1958a, 8)

In other words, what Arendt is saying is that the world is held in common not only with those who live presently in it but also with those who came before and those who will come after. So, we are responsible and culpable for our acts because we live among humans in the present and there will be others replacing us in the future. We can see here a strange form of empathy and empowerment which lives and struggles for the fulfilment of the present rather than for the hope of a utopian future. This is a life of choice (*hairetikos*) and risk (*kindunos*: κίνδυνοσ). In Greek tragedy, risk is always related to destiny. That is to say, heresy is not a path of salvation; it is an expression of destiny. In other words, in the creative work of the heretic, suffering and transformation replace arrogance and utopia. We can sense the difficulty here, for at the end the heretical actor cannot avoid the spirit of paradox in his search of a transcendent foundation for rebellion and dissent, but at the same time he/she has to transcend all transcendental foundations at some point in the name of the heretical imperative.

Therefore, the question is: how does the heretic thinker and creator transcend his/her self-interest in the name of genuine love for humanity? Surely, the instinctive rebellion of the heretic is related to this-worldliness of life itself. This exists because of an upsurge of the heretic's faith in the potentialities of human creativity and his/her profound sense of solidarity in the struggle against evil. Moreover, suffering remains a central value for the heretic, but in the sense that his/her personal heretical revolt and act of dissent are grounded in an experience common to all human beings. From this standpoint, in the tragic work of the heretical intellectual the centre of the stage is sought by a renewed fidelity to human moral conscience. If we take the example of Albert Camus here again, we can say that for him rebellion is essentially guided against absurdity, violence, and death. Metaphysical rebellion, underlines Camus, is 'the movement by which man protests against his condition and the whole creation of creation' (Camus 1956, 23). However, as a great champion of human dignity, Camus gave high priority to his denunciation of those forces of inhumanity that took the side of death simply because, for him, the ultimate injustice was the death penalty.

Not surprisingly, Camus identified his life and work with the abolition of capital punishment. As a matter of fact, the heretic battle of Camus, as a writer and a public intellectual, was a great example of all the battles of all heretics throughout history. Thus, Camus's trenchant critique of the guillotine was a way for him to defend the idea of fair and modest justice that did not have the pretension to present itself as a hideous punishment. The heretic critique of justice by Camus stands as a severe analysis of a society which claims the right to administer total punishment to a murderer without assuming any responsibility for the crimes. Camus's opposition to capital punishment was clearly derived from his highly heretical view of the society of his time in which human solidarity against death was denied. Meanwhile, accepting to live the limits of human nature without creating despair in the hearts of men was also a heretical effort by Camus to find a middle way between conformity and terror. As mentioned previously, if Camus is a typical representative of heretical intellectualism, it is because the entirety of his artistic, intellectual, and political engagements were based on the notion of rebellion against death, violence, and injustice. What Camus sought to demonstrate was that the betrayal of heresy in the contemporary world is closely related not only to the dehumanizing practices of the revolutionary tradition but also to the visceral contempt of the bourgeois society for Socratic questioning. 'Why rebel if there is nothing permanent in oneself

worth preserving?' (1956, 16) asks Camus in his majestic book
*The Rebel.* Camus's line of questioning takes us to an immediate
answer that heretical dissent is not essentially an egoistic movement. It is a revolt against the oppression and suffering of others.
However, it is also the raison d'être for humanity to fight against
the existence of evil in history.

It is never too late to glorify heretic resistance against the
presence of evil in history. It is never too late to fight violence
and hatred. So, if heresy is essentially the ethical dimension
of mankind—a principle of existence that aspires for common life—then it goes without saying that it engenders action
for creative transformation in historical battles against evil.
As such, the call to heresy is also a call to think, to create, and to
transform. Therefore, as mankind confronts conformism, complacency, and mediocrity, it resists thoughtlessness and at the
same time challenges evil. But the only way to defy and discard
thoughtlessness is through heretical intervention in the world.
Heresy manifests in us the spirit of dissent and disobedience so
that we do not succumb to meaninglessness. This means that we
can fight evil and transcend it. As Camus writes in *The Plague,*
this attitude makes 'truth flash forth from the dark cloud of
seeming injustice' (1948, 206). Once again we find ourselves
face to face with the three forms of injustice described by
Camus: violence, murder, and the death penalty.

More precisely, Camus's call to heresy is also a call to
humanize the world by preserving the ethical value of non-
violence. It is a fact that the critique of violence and the
search for non-violence run through Camus's writings and
can be viewed as essential for understanding his philosophy
of heresy. Originally, Camus's philosophical heresy seeks to

create a culture of non-violence that values the common humanity of all individuals and nations while being in harmony with the Earth. This is where the concept of the 'new Mediterranean culture' takes shape in Camus's philosophy. 'This culture,' affirms Camus, 'this Mediterranean truth, exists and shows itself all along the line. ... The Mediterranean gives us the picture of a living, highly colored, concrete civilization which changes doctrines into its own likeness and receives ideas without changing its own nature' (1968, 194–5). That is to say, for Camus, the heretic choice is to rehabilitate the Mediterranean as a culture of 'smiles, sea and sunlight' against the civilization of violence, murder, and injustice. He underlines, 'In the world of violence and death around us, there is no place for hope. But perhaps there is room for civilization, for real civilization, which puts truth before fables and life before dreams. And this civilization has nothing to do with hope. In it man lives on his truths' (1968, 197). Thus, Camus's heretical formulation of 'Mediterranean humanism' is consistent with his commitment to the otherness of the Other, which stands in opposition to historical necessity. Accordingly, in his *Letters to a German Friend*, Camus goes on to explain the differences that existed between the average Frenchman and the average German in the manner they approached, during the struggle against Nazism, the glory of their nation and the preservation of freedom. 'It is a great deal ... to face torture and death when you know for a fact that hatred and violence are empty things in themselves. It is a great deal to fight while despising war, to accept losing everything while still preferring happiness, to face destruction while cherishing the idea of a higher civilization' (Camus 1995c, 6–7). As such, the only

truth for Camus is the human urge to be free, not in the name
of a void heroism but in order to distinguish between 'the
man of the future and the cowardly gods' (Camus 1995c, 10).
Camus makes his point here that human beings need to dis-
regard the fear of death and act as free creatures. In being
grounded in human freedom, the heretical thinker or artist
carries the burden of fighting for all those who cannot defend
themselves against tyrannies. 'We must know,' points out
Camus, 'that we can never escape the common misery and
that our only justification, if indeed there is a justification, is
to speak up, insofar as we can, for those who cannot do so'
(Camus 1995b, 267).

Camus felt quite strongly that a heretical artist, writer, or
thinker is somebody who has to take a stand in favour of the
freedom of expression against all forms of intolerance which
endanger the very ground of thinking and creativity. Thus, in a
sense, heresy cannot serve anything but the freedom of human
beings by drawing them out of the spirit of tyranny and social
suffering. Camus's image of a heretical artist and writer is that
of a person 'who, in bearing witness to the common suffering
of humans in view of their ideal potentials, offers to them an
image of their dignity that ennobles the spirit in its common
struggles against a recalcitrant, indifferent universe' (Sprintzen
1988, 240). Here, we have the key to Camus's understanding
of heresy as an intellectual and artistic attitude rooted in the
notion of 'creating dangerously'. Here, Camus combines an artist's acute sense of commitment to beauty with a heretical urge
to revolt and freedom. Heresy, therefore, surges up between fate
and choice. To create is to choose to transform one's freedom
into fatality and one's heretical revolt into beauty. This view is

not a plea to engage in art but constitutes a heretical challenge to all forms of tyranny that restrict the freedom of creating. The heretical essence of Camus's work is well embodied in his defence of the idea of a free artist.

And art, by the virtue of that free essence I have tried to define, unites whereas tyranny separates. It is not surprising, therefore, that art should be the enemy marked out by every form of oppression. It is not surprising that artists and intellectuals should have been the first victims of modern tyrannies, whether of the Right or of the Left. Tyrants know there is in the work of art an emancipatory force, which is mysterious only to those who do not revere it. Every great work makes the human face more admirable and richer, and this is its whole secret. And thousands of concentration camps and barred cells are not enough to hide this staggering testimony of dignity. (Camus 1995b, 269–70)

In short, for Camus, heresy is a point of departure, not a conclusion. It is the conviction to which we must hold firm if we are to find our way out of meaninglessness. Obviously, Camus stands out as the heretical voice of his generation. By setting an example of maturity and explicitness, Albert Camus did leave behind a model of complacency and conformism. At the same time, howoever, when approaching the problems of thinking and creating, he went beyond the era of chair-bound artists. Thus, he achieved both in his work and in his personality a fair balance between a revolution of values and a reconstruction of a dialogical community. As he underlines in 'The Artist and His Time' from *The Myth of Sisyphus and Other Essays*:

Even if, militants in our lives, we speak in our work of deserts and of selfish love, the mere fact that our lives are militant causes a special tone of voice to people with men that desert and that

love. I shall certainly not choose the moment when we are beginning to leave nihilism behind to stupidly deny the values of creation in favor of the values of humanity, or vice versa. In my
mind neither one is ever separated from the other and I measure
the greatness of an artist (Moliere, Tolstoy, Melville) by the balance he managed to maintain between the two. Today, under the
pressure of events, we are obliged to transport that tension into
our lives likewise. This is why so many artists, bending under
the burden, take refuge in the ivory tower or, conversely, in the
social church. But as for me, I see in both choices a like act of
resignation. We must simultaneously serve suffering and beauty.
(Camus 1955, 150–1)

Camus's claim is the following: An assertion of the absolute
truth destroys the possibility of beauty. Faced with this, one must
have a heretical confrontation with ugliness and banality. That
would require the courage to die and an acute sense of beauty.
Albert Camus possessed both, so did Yukio Mishima.

# 3

## AESTHETICIZING HERESY
Death and Beauty

Yukio Mishima, perhaps the most influential Japanese writer of his time, was in many ways a heretic in search of authenticity. Mishima's quest for beauty and heroic death, a reflex of his heresy, could be seen as a clear symptom of his obsession with the gap between reality and the existential questions that he accounted of crucial human importance. Midway between violent sensuality and critical aestheticism, Mishima's words and actions hold the promise of a nonconformist beauty hand in hand with the quest for purity of the self. As Hisaaki Yamanouchi says correctly,

> Mishima's whole career was one of paradox built on an extraordinary tension between spirit and body, words and action, and artistic creation and commitment to the world. It is practically impossible for a man of lesser stature than Mishima himself to explain away the mater, and the following will be merely a modest attempt to trace the development of Mishima as a man and writer and to find the logical connexion, if any, between his aesthetics and its confrontation with the world which culminated in his suicide. (1972, 1)

Mishima believed in the deep wisdom of the Japanese philosophy of Bushido, which, from his point of view, has been undermined by the post–World War II Japan. In this respect, due to the Americanization of the Japanese society and the thoughtlessness of the Japanese masses, Mishima never spoke to those who did not have an ear to hear the unconformity and an eye to observe the beauty. As such, Mishima's heretical dissent turned into an aristocratic, elitist, and self-valorizing spirit, which took place on artistic grounds as a confrontation with the passivity and mediocrity of the surrounding world. Consequently, the forcefulness of Mishima's heretical dissent was reinforced by his alertness to what was happening around him and against his towering self-confidence. A sign of the latter appeared later in his life, especially through his adoption of the samurai ethos of living and thinking. This is perhaps more noticeable in Mishima's book *Sun and Steel*, where he praises the aesthetic value of the body with a gaze at the Greek concept of beauty. As he puts it,

> The theme of estrangement of body and spirit, born of the craving I have described, persisted for a long time as a principal theme in my work. I only came to take gradual leave of it when I at last began to consider whether it was not possible that the body, too, might have its own logic, possibly even its own thought; when I began to feel that the body's special qualities did not lie solely in taciturnity and beauty of form, but that the body too might have its own loquacity. (Mishima 1970, 17–18)

Mishima was one of the rare Japanese writers who found a balance between the Bushido and the Greek idealization of physical beauty. Moreover, for him the heretical ideal of heroic beauty was intertwined with the beauty of artistic creation.

This subversive symbiosis of the world of *poeisis* (creativity) and the world of praxis (action) translates in his writings into an acid power of words. Mishima's insatiable desire to unite the mind and the body is arguably manifest in his aesthetic and heretical approach to death. According to Peter Abelsen,

> The reality that Mishima tried to convey through his work was that of the struggle within himself between intellectuality and physicality. The anguish of that struggle brought forth the theme of a desire for purity, the development of which went hand in hand with his personal development from merely wanting to be true to himself (as represented by the search for personal identity in *Confessions of a Mask*), via the blossoming out of his morbid fascination (as represented by the bloody heroism of a Takeyama) to a ripened awareness of the ironic outcome of every quest for purity of the self (as represented by the crippled lust for glory of Isao). In the process, the line between the writer and his work blurred as his self-knowledge grew with the creation of ever subtler characters-until finally the inner reality which he had always put into his work flowed back from the pages into real life. (1966, 661)

The strengthening of Mishima's body turned him from a man of words into a man of swords. His obsession with a pure and aesthetic death turned the dialectic of *Sun and Steel* into a violent heretical revolt against the banality and mediocrity of the modern consumer society. The final act of aestheticization of this heretical revolt was his ritual death in November 1970 in the traditional samurai manner of *seppuku* (ritualistic suicide) after a vain attempt to prepare a coup d'état with a unit of the Japanese Self-Defence Forces. By dying in a manner of a Japanese warrior, Mishima tried to bring his heretical revolt in line with his aesthetic vision. He once said, 'Dying for a great cause was considered the most glorious, heroic, and brilliant way of dying.'[1] Though many still contest Mishima's dramatic death as an act of lunacy, we have to admit that it was not only heroic but also mainly heretical in essence. Actually, Mishima's heretical dissent was not that of an intellectual agitator but that of a rebellious aesthete, who knew how to unveil the bourgeoning nihilism of contemporary culture. His heretical challenge of the post-World War II Japanese society was most probably an invitation to a painful self-examination and dismissal of conventional solutions. Mishima's best response to the crisis of existential hopelessness and despair in Japan was to overcome it by the power of words. It was through the power of words that he transformed himself into the master of both realms of creativity and physicality. Through this self-awareness of his body, Mishima learned not to deny death but to confront it with beauty. In a nutshell, he 'maintained a harmonious balance between intellect and flesh' (Wagenaar and Iwamoto 1975, 45). All of his work and his suicide, so intimately linked with it, can be seen from a position of intensity of emotions rather than a position of rationality.

It goes without saying that Mishima's literary world is aesthetically intense and emotionally erotic. These two elements compose a heretic vision of reality in his art of novel, which presents a venue of heroic escape from the decadence of modern Japan. This vision is always present in his writings in combination with references to elements of traditional Japanese beauty. To create

[1] See https://www.makingqueerhistory.com/articles/2017/10/1/yukio-mishima, last accessed on 23 July 2020.

an alternate world, he consciously adds fantasy and eroticism to his aesthetically filled romantic novels. This is a world where mediocrity, conformism, and complacency play no part. In this regard, it is especially significant that his heretical revolt against the Americanization of Japan consistently highlights the loss of Japanese innocence and authenticity. As it turns out, Mishima's highly heretical gaze of the Japanese society is an alternative vision which includes entire worlds of beauty, death, eroticism, and freedom. As such, his aesthetic–erotic literature is obsessive and antagonistic toward social and political institutions. He both expresses of post-war Japan and transcends it by providing a literary means which separates him from the straitjacket of tradition. That is why, many of his works have autobiographical elements in them and are written in a confessional style, being the so-called 'I novel' (*shishōsetsu*). Overall, his entangled relationship with heresy, artistic creativity, eroticism, and death translates to an atmosphere of confrontation and rejection of the emptiness of the Japanese society. Even more confrontational was Mishima's homosexuality that disturbed the normality of the Japanese public. At first glance, his homosexuality appears as more than a simple sexual orientation. Though married and father to several children, Mishima's elitist and heretic-centred world seems marginalized by his homosexuality and by his heretic–aesthetic engagements.

Not surprisingly, what distinguishes Mishima from many other Japanese writers of his time is that his confrontational and outcast character represents a heroic experience of lived heresy. It is in such a context that his political activities—starting in the mid-1960s when he put together his private army, the so-called Shield Society, in order to protect the emperor—and his ritual *seppuku* in November 1970 at Ichigaya represent heretical modes of confronting the mediocrity of the Japanese consumer society of his time. However, the most Mishimaesque sense of revolt against conformism and mediocrity is neither his sexual marginality nor his ritualistic suicide, but the heretical elements underlying his writings expressed by a search for authenticity. Much of his heretical existentialism is also a quest for an authentic self. One might better argue that his literary work shows strong traces of romanticism. The very fact of his choice to die for the divine status of the emperor and the samurai code was romantic heresy taken to its very limit: an attempt to achieve the purity of the tragic hero. For him, pain and physical courage were proofs of the unity of body and mind. The reason for this is simple: already in a note dated 2 November 1948, Mishima informed his editor that his plan was to 'turn upon [himself] the scalpel of psychological analysis' (cited in Nathan 1974, 94). Therefore, Mishima's lust for beauty and death turned into a heretical tendency to go beyond every mental ghetto while thinking through every experience in life. His work clearly shows that the convergence of the subjective and the objective takes place in a synthesis of art and reality. In his seminal essay *Sun and Steel*, Mishima explains why tragedy is, in his eyes, the highest level of heretical existence. He writes:

> According to my definition of tragedy, the tragic pathos is born when the perfectly average sensibility momentarily takes unto itself a privileged nobility that keeps others at a distance, and not when a special type of sensibility vaunts its own special claims. It follows that he who dabbles in words can create tragedy, but cannot participate in it. It is necessary, moreover, that the 'privileged nobility' find its basis strictly in a kind of physical

courage. The elements of intoxication and super human clarity in the tragic are born when the average sensibility, endowed with a given physical strength, encounters that type of privileged moment especially designed for it. Tragedy calls for an anti-tragic vitality and ignorance, and above all for a certain 'inappropriateness'. If a person is at times to draw close to the divine, then under normal conditions he must be neither divine nor anything approaching it. (Mishima 1970, 14–15)

Heretical heroism comes only to those who have the courage to go beyond reality with the agency of action and words. We can find further examples of Mishima's obsession with tragedy in the obsession of his heroes with death as a way of giving meaning to beauty, to love, and to life itself. If there is only one story of his which represents the essence of the spiritual force of his heretical imperative, it is 'Yukoku' ('Patriotism'). In this story, Mishima deals with the coup d'état of 26 February 1936.

What Mishima decided to do in 'Yukoku' was to describe what is not at all mentioned in the original count: the reality of such 'excellent' and 'admirable' deaths. ... Mishima wrote: 'The story of "Yukoku" itself is no more than an official part of the 2.26 Incident, but the spectacle of love and death, the perfect melding and potentiation of Eros and *taigi* [great cause, moral law, or justice] described here, is the only bliss I expect in this life.' (Inose and Sato 2012, 372, 374)

The protagonist of 'Patriotism' is Lieutenant Takeyama, an officer stationed in Tokyo during the coup d'état, who is ordered to resist the rebels. But he is a friend of the rebel officers and cannot follow the orders to arrest them. Therefore, he decides to go back home and commit *seppuku*. In this story, Mishima describes in detail the scene of the young man's *seppuku* in front of his young wife. By idealizing the act of *seppuku* as a result of the force of will and integrity of a heroic personality, Mishima anticipates his own practice of heretical heroism which ended with his act of disembowelment. Unsurprisingly enough, Mishima not only endorses the bravery and purity of the rebel officers of 1936 but also portrays Takeyama as a mythical hero of ancient Greece who attains happiness by choosing to die next to his wife. Mishima describes this desire for death in the sphere of beauty, love, and action with a great power of words and images:

> By the time the lieutenant had at last drawn the sword across to the right side of the stomach, the blade was already cutting shallow and had revealed its naked tip, slippery with blood and grease. But, suddenly stricken by a fit of vomiting, the lieutenant cried out hoarsely. The vomiting made the fierce pain fiercer still, and the stomach, which had thus far remained firm and compact, now abruptly heaved, opening wide its wound, and the entrails burst through, as if the wound too were vomiting. Seemingly ignorant of their master's suffering, the entrails gave an impression of robust health and almost disagreeable vitality as they slipped out smoothly and spilled over into the crotch. The lieutenant's head drooped, his shoulders heaved, his eyes opened to narrow slits, and a thin trickle of saliva dribbled from his mouth. The gold markings on his epaulets caught the light and glinted. Blood was scattered everywhere. ('Patriotism' by Mishima, cited in Scott-Stokes 1974, 233)

Mishima took his act of heretical aestheticism to the extreme by making a film version of 'Patriotism' and playing the role of Lieutenant Shinji Takeyama in it. In retrospect, one can look at this short film as a rehearsal of the future suicide of Mishima and as a testament to his entire literary and artistic work. However, according to Edward Seidensticker, a specialist of Mishima's works,

> the most apposite rehearsal comes in *Sea of Fertility*. The tetralogy covers a sweep in time from before the First World War down to yesterday. Formally, it centers upon the theme of reincarnation, which Mishima has told us he borrowed from a late-Heian romance. In the second of its reincarnations, the protagonistic ectoplasm is made manifest in the person and deeds of a young man who, in the fevered patriotism of the Thirties, does not hesitate to do violence for what seems to him right. Toward the end of the second volume, he is on trial for having participated in an abortive attempt at righteous violence. Under examination by the presiding judge, he explains his motives at length, and the resemblance to Mishima's own statement scarcely requires comment:

> Yes. I wanted to carry out the principle of the unity of knowledge and action, the main principle of the school of Wang Yang-Ming: 'To know and not to act is not yet to know.' Knowing of the corruption around us, of the dark clouds that close off the future of Japan, the poverty of farm villages and the sufferings of the poor; knowing that the origins of it all are in corrupt government and in an irresponsible moneyed class whose interests are served by the corruption; knowing that these are the roots of the growth that cuts off the light of His Revered and Benevolent Majesty: knowing all this, I find it evident that to know is to act. (Seidensticker 1971, 275)

It will seem here, perhaps, that too much is being made of Mishima's actions. But the steel changed him from a weak young man with erotico-aesthetic phantasies into a self-affirmed and hardened heretic. 'The strengthening of Mishima's body had indeed an effect on his mind, though not that of inducing a classic universality but of letting him feel, rather than imagine, what Death and Blood would actually be like' (Abelsen 1966, 661). As noted, the heretical essence of Mishima's life and work consists of a symbiosis of various dimensions, reflecting his rebellious Weltanschauung, the main philosophical constituents being heroic consciousness and tragic sensitivity. In metaphysical terms, there is, in Mishima, a heretical transcendence of the duality of body and mind through spilt blood. According to Henry Scott-Stokes,

> Blood gave him a sexual thrill—this was one of his most important 'confessions' and the core of his aesthetics. The beauty of the spilt blood of the samurai has been endlessly poeticized by the Japanese, who liken the short-lived blossom of the cherry tree to the life of the samurai. Mishima, however, romanticized death and blood in a manner foreign to the Japanese classical tradition. (1974, 83)

In Mishima's philosophy of life and death, blood was ultimately a heretical element. As such, he was influenced both by the classical traditions of Japan and by the 'murder theatre' literature of the West. Among the novels which influenced him in relation to this subject was *Quo Vadis* written by Henryk Sienkiewicz in Polish and translated into English. This is how he describes his reading of *Quo Vadis* in a partly autobiographical work entitled *Confessions of a Mask*:

> My inherent deficiency of blood had first implanted in me the impulse to dream of bloodshed. And in its turn that impulse had caused me to lose more and more of the stuff of blood from my body, thereby further increasing my lust for blood. This enfeebling life of dreaming sharpened and exercised my imagination.

Although I was not yet acquainted with the works of De Sade, the description of the Colosseum in *Quo Vadis* had made a deep impression on me, and by myself I had dreamed up the idea of a murder theatre. (1958, 92)

Mishima's fascination with death and blood had not only a romantic essence but also a tragic frame. This was what he called a 'true antithesis of words' and contained in his mind a true image of Japan with the emperor at the centre. In Mishima's heretical mind, the shame of Japan's surrender to the United States of America (USA) in World War II pointed to a crisis of meaning in the Japanese society. Like a hero of *The Forty–Seven Ronin*, the epic tale of Japan, centred around '*giri* [duty] to one's lord', Mishima felt that the Japanese society had failed because it allowed consumerism and liberalism to obscure its obligations of *giri*. For him, the dilemma of virtue was to choose between shame and self-discipline. He chose the second through a life of writing and intensive physical training. He transformed his sense of shame into a nobility of spirit, which is a sign of a true heretic mind.

One can make sense of Mishima's final heroic act only if one assumes that his ultimate purpose was of a heretical nature: choosing to die theatrically in order to give meaning to his life in a meaningless world. Many were repelled by his *seppuku*, others were deeply moved. He knew that others would not understand the true meaning of his death. Heresy is never understood by un-heretical masses. In a conversation which he had with another Japanese novelist, Jun Ishikawa, a few weeks before the Ichigaya incident, Mishima pointed to this misunderstanding: 'I come out on the stage determined to make the audience weep and instead they burst out laughing' (cited in Scott-Stokes 1974, 312).

If Mishima were alive today, he would perhaps be just as disappointed at the Japanese consumerist society as he was back in November 1970, when he committed the ritualistic suicide. However, if he had to live, he would also be engaged in an all-out struggle against a world where the nobility of spirit is reduced to the mediocrity of fame. One should not conclude, however, that Yukio Mishima spent his life worrying about being a celebrity. On the contrary, he opted for a glory which was that of a heretic, against gods and the masses. 'I want to identify my literary work with God,' Mishima affirmed once to an extreme right-wing militant. Perhaps he was reminded of one of his favourite heretic philosophers, Friedrich Nietzsche, who said: 'He who has a why to live can bear almost any how' (cited in Scott-Stokes 1974, 203).

# II
## THE HERETICAL INDIAN

# 4

# AMBEDKAR AND THE HERETICAL IMPERATIVE

Of all the heretic thinkers and artists discussed in this book, B.R. Ambedkar may have had the most complex relationship with the idea of heresy. He certainly followed neither any gods nor any masses. In that sense, he was an autonomous individual who took his destiny in his own hands. Unlike Mishima, he had no necrophilic or aesthetic vision of life. Likewise, as opposed to Camus who believed that humans live in a world that is indifferent to their sufferings, Ambedkar's philosophy of existence was oriented toward the end of suffering as a social curse. Ambedkar fought against untouchability throughout his career. For him, the struggle for democracy in India was an act of heretical imperative. 'Democracy,' he wrote, 'is not merely a form of government. It is primarily a mode of associated living of conjoint communicated experience. It is essentially an attitude of respect and reverence towards fellowmen' (Ambedkar 1995, 55). This statement of Ambedkar not only shows his faith in the historical progress of liberty but also expresses his ethics of empathy for the social emancipation of his fellow Indians. However, more than being

a simple dreamer who would give false hopes to the oppressed
populations of India, Ambedkar was a heretic who, in his own
words, acted as 'the scourge and the scavenger of the society'
(cited in Sakrikar 1992, 169). This was Ambedkar's definition
of a great man. However, for him, a great man was not necessarily a great hero. Generally speaking, Ambedkar, the heretic, was
against the cult of the hero. He did not want to be considered a
hero, as was the case with Gandhi, Jinnah, or Nehru. That is why
he distinguished between the 'sense of admiration' and 'hero
worship'. He observed:

> Hero worship in the sense of expressing our unbounded admira-
> tion is one thing. To obey the hero is a totally different kind of
> worship. There is nothing wrong in the former while the lat-
> ter is no doubt a most pernicious thing. The former is man's
> respect for which is noble and of which the great men are only
> an embodiment. The latter is the serf's fealty to his lord. The for-
> mer is consistent with respect, but the latter is a sign of debase-
> ment. The former does not take away one's intelligence to think
> and independence to act. The latter makes one perfect fool. The
> former involves no disaster to the state. The latter is a source of
> positive danger to it. (Ambedkar 1979, 231)

Ambedkar's criticism is clearly addressed to Gandhi and
Jinnah whose followers discredited and condemned him. But
Ambedkar was clear about his personal feelings and political
judgments concerning Gandhi and Jinnah. On 15 March 1943,
in a preface to his essay 'Ranade, Gandhi and Jinnah', he wrote
the following:

> However strong and however filthy be the abuses which the
> Congress Press chooses to shower on me, I must do my duty.
> I am no worshipper of idols. I believe in breaking them. I insist

that if I hate Mr. Gandhi and Mr. Jinnah—I dislike them, I do not hate them—it is because I love India more. That is the true faith of a nationalist. I have hopes that my countrymen will some day learn that the country is greater than the men, that the worship of Mr. Gandhi or Mr. Jinnah and service to India are two very different things and may even be contradictory of each other. (Ambedkar 1979, 209)

Ambedkar was not a nationalist in the everyday sense of the term. For him, a nation was not just a collection of citizens. It represented a special mode of living and communicating. As he stated, 'A nation is not a country in the physical sense, whatever degree of geographical unity it may possess. A nation is not a people synthesized by a common culture derived from common language, common religion or common race. ... Nationality is a subjective psychological feeling' (Ambedkar 1979, 223). As Aloysius underlines, Ambedkar considered nationalism as a 're-organization of social relations within a culture and claim for separate existence to maintain this new social configuration, that is, democratization and popular sovereignty. ... His idea of the nation revolved around the creation of a modern political community of free and equal individuals as citizens' (2017, 155). As such, Ambedkar refuted the cultural and racial nationalism of those who abided by the Hindu ideal of *varna-vyavastha* (governance through caste system). Drawing heavily on the modern European idea of democracy, particularly what he knew about the French Revolution, Ambedkar criticized the Brahmanical notion that individuals were born differently by pointing to the fact that Brahmanism and democracy could not go together. Accordingly, Ambedkar believed that Hinduism did not recognize the value of fraternity because of the hierarchical nature of its caste system. Unlike Gandhi, Ambedkar did not distinguish between the caste and the varna system. According to him, they were founded on the same principle and state of mind. He observed:

> Reformers working for the removal of untouchability, including Mahatma Gandhi, do not seem to realize that the acts of the people are merely the results of their beliefs inculcated upon their mind by the Shastras and that people will not change their conduct until they cease to believe in the sanctity of the Shastras on which their conduct is founded. (Cited in Mungekar 2017, 91)

In Ambedkar's view, the Hindu society was cursed by the privileges given to the Brahmins, whom he called the 'Supermen', against those with no privilege at all. However, he saw the evil of the Hindu society not only in Brahmanism but also in the undemocratic structure of the varnas. He argued, 'The Hindu social system is undemocratic not by accident. It is designed to be undemocratic. Its division of society into varnas and castes, and of castes and outcastes are not theories but are decrees. They are all barricades raised against democracy' (Ambedkar 1987, volume 4, 284). According to Ambedkar, the anti-democratic nature of Brahmanism was crystallized by the fact that Brahmins represented the intellectual class in a Hindu society. As a result, 'When such an intellectual class, which holds the rest of the community in its grip, is opposed to the reform of Caste, the chances of success in a movement for the break-up of the Caste system appear to me very, very remote' (Ambedkar 1979, 71). To prove this point, Ambedkar quoted broadly the Hindu religious texts in his writings. He tried to show the inegalitarian effects of the caste system in the Indian society. But his aim, as a heretic, was also to demonstrate ways to go beyond this injustice. His work on the 'Annihilation of Caste' was a critical reflection on the possibilities of social justice in India. As Ananya Vajpeyi points out, Ambedkar's

> struggle for justice, for a new social and political order founded on the principles of liberty, equality, and fraternity, was consubstantial with his life itself. His final conversion to Buddhism was not a freakish deviation from this path: all that had happened was that he could at last see how duhkha and inequality converged at a vanishing point, in the far distance where the social and the religious merge to yield the political. The independence of India, the conversion of Untouchables into Buddhists, and the transformation of Indian society such that the prison house of caste gave way to an emancipating principle of equal citizenship: these were all simultaneous and necessary conditions for the true achievement of an Indic modernity. (Vajpeyi 2012, 236–7)

As a matter of fact, while addressing the questions of graded inequality and fixity of occupation in the Indian caste system, Ambedkar was also very attentive to the question of democracy. He remarked: 'You must give a new doctrinal basis to your Religion—a basis that will be in consonance with Liberty, Equality and Fraternity, in short, with Democracy' (Ambedkar 1979, 77).

Ambedkar's negative attitude towards Brahmanical hegemony can be explained as a general criticism addressed to power politics, which he considered as a legacy of British colonialism in India. In all and for all, Ambedkar wanted the new Indian agenda to take note of the social and political emancipation of Indians as modern citizens of a democracy rather than privileging the Brahmanical power base as the driving force of the Indian society. It is in this sense that Ambedkar's heretical critique of the Brahmanic historiography represents a revolutionary attempt to defy the sanctity of the Hindu religion and its hegemonic narrative. According to Anuradha Mukherjee:

> In fact, it was for the first time in Indian history that defiance took a multi-pronged approach. ... Dr. Ambedkar and his intellect to shatter the age-old cultural myth and the sanctions imposed by an elitist political order on the millions of Indian's poor downtrodden deprived masses and give them real human rights and power that they deserved like any other people in the world. Ambedkar visioned the political rise of the Untouchables. (Mukherjee 2015, 168)

Unlike Gandhi, Ambedkar considered religion, more specifically Hinduism, as the embodiment of social inequality and injustice. But his approach to Hinduism was more than that of a simple social reformer. Though he felt that religion is an essential part of life, he tried to extirpate what he considered as outdated practices and repressive measures of Brahmanism. Simultaneously, he regarded religion as a value system which could be part of the process of nation-building in India. But since he rejected both the system of hierarchy and the theory of God, his heretic ideas on religion transcended the unique dimension of spirituality and were more inclined towards the concept of civic unity in a democratic civilization. In an address delivered at Solapur during the Matang Conference on 4 January 1938, he developed what he understood by the concept of 'democratic civilization'. He asserted,

> This is a war between democracy and dictatorship—not an enlightened dictatorship but a dictatorship of the most barbarous character based not on any moral ideal but on racial

arrogance. If any dictatorship needs to be destroyed it is this vile Nazi dictatorship. Amidst all the political dissensions that one witnesses in this country ... we are likely to forget what a menace to our future this Nazism, if it wins, is going to be. What is more important is that its racial basis is a positive danger to Indians. ... There lies on us a very heavy duty to see that democracy does not vanish from the earth as a governing principle of human relationship. If we believe in it, we must be both true and loyal to it. We must not only be staunch in our faith in democracy but we must resolve to see that in whatever we do, we don not help the enemies of democracy to uproot the principles of liberty, equality and fraternity. ... If democracy lives, we are sure to reap the fruits of it. If democracy dies, it will be our doom. (Jaffrelot and Kumar 2018, 77–8)

As we can see, Ambedkar was no simple opponent to Hinduism. His heretical attitude was both towards the non-egalitarian attitudes of modern politics and towards the non-modern categories of selfhood in the Indian society. 'Ambedkar understood that when most Indians, especially Hindus, looked at their new flag or their new currency, they were not thinking of ancient Buddhists or contemporary Untouchables, nor were they experiencing a newfound faith in egalitarianism and compassion for the downtrodden' (Vajpeyi 2012, 241). It should be noted that Ambedkar's attitude toward tradition was very different from that of Mahatma Gandhi, Maulana Azad, Jawaharlal Nehru, and Sardar Patel. He did not intervene in tradition; he criticized it while recognizing its importance. As such, his desire to build a new India as an inclusive republic went hand in hand with his heretical revolt against the mechanism of hierarchy and the system of caste. 'This new India—whose key text, the Constitution of 1950, Ambedkar shepherded into its inaugural form—had to be imagined on the basis of a kind of selfhood that would appeal as much to Hindus as to minorities, to upper castes as to Sudras and Untouchables, and to those in the mainstream as to those on the margins' (Vajpeyi 2012, 209).

As far as we can decipher, Ambedkar's heretical mindset derives not only from his social and political sufferings as an Untouchable but mainly from his intellectual self-governance, which defines his mode of being as a dissenter in the Indian society. Indeed, it is important to note the philosophical context in which Ambedkar's heretical view is bound with his critique of the politics of the public sphere in India. Ambedkar's engagement with the caste system as a jurist, a politician, and an intellectual was much deeper than just a controversial debate with Mahatma Gandhi. Consequently, Ambedkar's heretical imperative of change in the Indian society was to deconstruct and destroy the caste system as the normative backbone of social and political inequalities.

> The solution that Ambedkar proposed was the annihilation of caste. He suggested inter-caste marriage and inter-dining for the purpose, although the latter by itself is too weak to forge any enduring bonds. Further, he felt that hereditary priesthood should go and it should remain open to all the co-religionists endowed with appropriate qualifications as certified by the state. (Rodrigues 2002, 'Introduction', 26–7)

Ambedkar's arguments against casteism and Hinduism almost echo the arguments of Martin Luther King, Jr, against segregation in the USA, with one major difference: Ambedkar cannot be considered a man of God in the same way as Martin Luther King, Jr, because the latter was a Baptist reverend and a follower of Jesus Christ. Unlike Dr King, Ambedkar was a heretical critic of religion and also a true social anatomist of it. As Rodrigues points out correctly:

> Ambedkar acknowledged the power of religion and upheld its need, but there is no place in his religion for God and the transcendent. He subscribed to a secular religion, moving away from established religions geared towards the sacred *vis-à-vis* the profane. His writings reveal a deep sensitivity to religion, much before his enchantment with Buddhism. He felt that since human beings are part of this world, the primary role of religion is to safeguard the moral domain. (2002, 19)

Actually, Ambedkar's approach to religion is more that of the annexation of religion by politics for its own purposes. In this Ambedkarian dialogue between religion and politics, it is not the religion that is empowered but the citizenship that is inflated and strengthened. Ambedkar's renouncement of Hinduism and his act of embracing Buddhism is not for the sake of religion in general but a gesture of enhancing good citizenship. In a text entitled 'Conversion', Ambedkar explains his position on the social and non-theological function of religion. He affirms:

> The force of the argument, of course, rests on a view of religion which is somewhat different from the ordinary view according to which religion is concerned with man's relation to God and all that it means. According to this view religion exists not for the saving of souls but for the preservation of society and the welfare of the individual. It is only those who accept the former view of religion that find it difficult to understand how conversion can solve the problem of untouchability. Those who accept the view of religion adopted in this chapter will have no difficulty in accepting the soundness of the conclusion. (Rodrigues 2002, 238)

Therefore, Ambedkar's approach to religion is purely from the point of view of civic friendship. In other words, the basis of conversion for him is to find a space and opportunity for accessing positive rights. According to this argument, Ambedkar should be classified as a 'civil religion' theorist, especially because there are traces of liberal thought in his political philosophy. Hence, it may well be that we need to appreciate the heretic nature of Ambedkar's thinking in its long struggle against Hindu orthodoxy and Brahmin power in the larger picture of the domestication of religion by civic republicanism. Actually, Ambedkar does go all the way with a civic–republican vision of political community by rejecting Hindutva's self-affirmation of the 'chosen castes' and exclusion of the downtrodden. If this is the case, then Ambedkar's support for a full-bodied civic republicanism can be defined as the civilizing process of Hinduism. Here again, Ambedkar is the only founding father of independent India to confront Hinduism on his own terms, which is to oppose the radicalness of the heretical imperative with the threat that Hinduism as a social religion poses to the integrity of civic life. Ambedkar's acknowledgement of the truth of his heretic project of defending the Indian public sphere against the dogmatism and intolerance of the dominant religion (that is, Hinduism) teaches us that we must be resolute in resisting any form of theocratic politics. We can draw a temporary conclusion from this Ambedkarian standpoint and add that Ambedkar teaches us that the inward freedom of the mind can always resist all forms of conformity and immaturity. This is more than evident in the role he played in the Indian Constitution–making process.

For Ambedkar, participating in the drafting of the Indian Constitution was the greatest antidote to the poison of religious intolerance and superstition. In taking up the responsibility of drafting independent India's Constitution, Ambedkar had undoubtedly tried to focus on promoting civic republicanism against any form of religious sacralization of the Indian state. In a Machiavellian manner, Ambedkar understood that pure republican virtue only works by asserting the rights of citizens before the rights of those who take an oath of allegiance to a religion (here, Hinduism). For Ambedkar, the problem was to align himself with a form of spirituality that itself fully embodied civic autonomy and equality, as opposed to the many instantiations of religious belief and practice that are non-egalitarian and heteronomous. While Ambedkar insisted on the social significance of religion in public life, he strongly refuted that all religions are egalitarian. He, thus, diagnosed Hinduism as a religion of inequality because it sanctified caste, and converted to Buddhism with his followers because he considered it a more just and righteous religion. Following the heretical imperative, Ambedkar pursued the idea that if religion has its source in moral conscience, then we can evolve ways of being religious in our own rational and moral capacities. In that sense, civic republicanism is the comprehensive doctrine to which Ambedkar commits himself to render his heretical philosophy fully coherent. However, it goes without saying that interpreting Ambedkar's heretical role in Indian politics in this way entails a radical intensification of the organization of public life in India as being quite challenging and unordinary. In short, Ambedkar believed that the Untouchables, to fulfill their humanity, need to be inspired by what John Stuart Mill called the 'height of inspiration'. Rather than saying, like Gandhi, that only 'ahimsa' and 'truth' can confer upon the Untouchables an absolutely exalted sense of purpose and hope, Ambedkar suggested conversion to Buddhism as a mode of redeeming the curse of being born a Dalit in a Hindu-majority society.

Ambedkar was clearly aware of his limits as a Dalit who had never been a member of the Congress Party, but also as a rare anti-colonial leader who dared criticize nationalism at the height of India's nationalist movement. Yet, every single learned Indian knows that the Indian Constitution was conceptualized by B.R. Ambedkar and not by Gandhi, Nehru, or Patel. In 1947, Ambedkar had the privilege of heading the seven-member drafting committee of the Constituent Assembly. That same year, Prime Minister Nehru invited Ambedkar to be the law minister of the new government. However, the cabinet's and the Parliament's rejection of Ambedkar's effort to reform the Hindu common law framework through a uniform civil code made him resign from the cabinet in 1951.

Ambedkar's Hindu Code Bill was a landmark and politically controversial document in its time. It was a mark of heresy coming from a Dalit in a country where Hindus constituted the majority of the population. For Ambedkar, the aim of this bill was to promote inter-caste marriages and provide some social justice by protecting those marginalized from the means of production and equal opportunities in the society. As it is mentioned in this document, 'Marriage under the Bill will be valid irrespective of the caste or sub-caste of the parties entering into the marriage' (Rodrigues 2002, 499). Unsurprisingly, both in the Hindu Code Bill and in the Indian Constitution, Ambedkar was not only concerned with the upliftment and empowerment of the oppressed classes of India but was also trying to provide a remedy for the inequality in Indian society. Both these texts, as his other writings, reflect that Ambedkar was highly inspired by the thinkers of the Enlightenment and by the ideas developed during the French Revolution. For example, in his essay 'Annihilation of Caste', Ambedkar affirms the following:

If you ask me, my ideal would be a society based on *Liberty*, *Equality* and *Fraternity*. And why not? What objection can there be to Fraternity? I cannot imagine any. An ideal society should be mobile, should be full of channels for conveying a change taking place in one part to other parts. In an ideal society there should be many interests consciously communicated and shared. ... Any objection to equality? This has obviously been the most contentious part of the slogan of the French Revolution. The objections to equality may be sound, and one may have to admit that all men are not equal. But what of that? Equality may be a fiction, but nonetheless one must accept it as the governing principle. A man's power is dependent upon (1) physical heredity; (2) social inheritance or endowment in the form of parental care, education, accumulation of scientific knowledge, everything which enables him to be more efficient than the savage; and finally, (3) on his own efforts. In all these three respects men are undoubtedly unequal. ... On the other hand, it can be urged that if it is good for the social body to get the most out of its members, it can get the most out of them only by making them equal as far as possible at the very start of the race. That is one reason why we cannot escape equality. But there is another reason why we must accept equality. A statesman is concerned with vast numbers of people. He has neither the time nor the knowledge to draw fine distinctions and to treat each one equitably, i.e. according to need or according to capacity. However desirable or reasonable an equitable treatment of men may be, humanity is not capable of assortment and classification. The statesman, therefore, must follow some rough and ready rule, and that rough and ready rule is to treat all men alike, not because they are alike but because classification and assortment is impossible. The doctrine of equality is glaringly fallacious but, taking all in all, it is the only way a statesman can proceed in politics—which is a severely practical affair and which demands a severely practical test. (Rodrigues 2002, 276–7)

This passage clearly shows to what extent Ambedkar's radical views were influenced by his readings of pre- and post-revolutionary France. His appropriation of the French Revolution is more symbolic than ideological. Given the fact that Ambedkar felt close to modern philosophy and was suspicious of every doctrine which bonded with myths, traditions, and religions, his assertion of the autonomy of the individual went hand in hand with his heretical rejection of a personal God and revelation. Ambedkar underlines:

That today God has taken the place of magic, does not alter the fact that God's place in religion is only as a means for the conservation of life and the end of religion is the conservation and consecration of social life. … The correct view is that religion like language is social for the reason that either is essential for social life and the individual has to have it because without it he cannot participate in the life of the society. (Rodrigues 2002, 225)

Consequently, Ambedkar did not think of religion and Indianness in equal terms. This equation between religion and identity had come to be universalized through colonial rule. In the long run, Ambedkar saw himself and the Untouchables confronted with a form of religious nationalism developed by many of his contemporaries who were involved in the Indian Independence movement. Therefore, Ambedkar's critique of Hinduism was considered by many of his contemporaries as an attack against Indian nationalism. Next to Rabindranath Tagore, Ambedkar is one of the rare Indian intellectuals of the pre-Independence period who dared to criticize openly the idea of nationalism. In an essay entitled 'Is There a Case for Pakistan?' (in *A Nation Calling For a Home*), he openly distinguishes between the two concepts of 'nationality' and 'nationalism'. Nationality means 'consciousness of kind, awareness of the existence of that tie of kinship'. Nationalism means 'the desire for a separate national existence for those who are bound by this tie of kinship' (cited in Ambedkar 2017). Second, it is true that nationalism cannot exist without there being the feeling of nationality. However, it is important to bear in mind that the converse is not always true. The feeling of nationality may be present, yet the feeling of nationalism may be quite absent. That is to say, nationality does not in all cases produce nationalism. For nationality to flame into nationalism, two conditions must exist. First, there must arise the 'will to live as a nation'. Nationalism is the dynamic expression of that desire. Second, there must be a territory which nationalism can occupy and make into a state as well as a cultural home of the nation. Without such a territory, nationalism, to use Lord Acton's phrase, would be a 'soul as it were wandering in search of a body in which to begin life over again and dies out finding none' (Rodrigues 2002, 468–9). As we can see clearly, Ambedkar remained wary of nationalism dominating the regime of rights. Once again, he was primarily concerned with civic republicanism rather than with national populism. However, he placed great emphasis on what he called the 'will to live as a nation' and remained critical of both the Congress and the Muslim League for precipitating the volitional factor against all forms of conviviality and coexistence in a single state. As a result, while trying to underplay the concept of nationalism, Ambedkar looked towards the sustainability and respect of rights as a solution to the problem of identities in the Indian society.

Further, Ambedkar's strong awareness of the rule of law posited itself as a heretical imperative toward the empowerment of a vibrant civil society and the permanence of dissent. Ambedkar pensively and compassionately inserted the anti-discrimination law in Chapter 3 of the Indian Constitution, dealing with Fundamental Rights. Undoubtedly, the heretical vision of Ambedkar is present in Articles 14, 15, and 17 mentioned in the Constitution of India. Article 14 declares that 'the State shall not deny to any person equality before the laws or the equal protection of the laws within the territory of India' (Constitution of India, Art. 14).[1] As for Article 15, it prohibits discrimination on the bases of religion, caste, race, sex, or place of birth. Finally, Article 17 represents the most heretical move made by Ambedkar in the Indian Constitution, which abolishes untouchability and outlaws its practice in any form. This clearly shows that Ambedkar considered 'habits of constitutional morality' as an important factor in his approach to civic republicanism, because it implies that using others against their will in order to achieve one's end is immoral since it violates their dignity as persons. This Kantian approach of Ambedkar is accomplished by another of his heretical moves as an *Aufklärer*, in the direction of Kant's definition of *Aufklärung* as man's release from his 'self-incurred tutelage'. As in the case of Kant and other philosophers

---

[1] Available at https://www.india.gov.in/my-government/constitution-india/constitution-india-full-text. Last accessed on 14 August 2020.

of the Enlightenment, Ambedkar believed that the downtrodden of India should take their destiny into their own hands and set their rights as the ultimate goal of their acts. In Ambedkar's mind, the autonomous destiny of the moral person put forward by the philosophers of the Enlightenment had nothing to do with the fixed destiny of the Hindu religion. In one of his writings on untouchability, Ambedkar comes back to this distinction in an essay entitled 'Outside the Fold' and affirms:

> This established order is a hereditary order both in status as well as in function. Once a Touchable, always a Touchable. Once an Untouchable, always an Untouchable. Once a Brahmin, always a Brahmin. Once a sweeper, always a sweeper. Under it, those who are born high, remain high; those who are born low, remain low. ... This destiny has no relation to the merits of the individuals living under it. An Untouchable however superior he may be mentally and morally, is below a Touchable in rank, no matter how inferior he may be mentally or morally. A Touchable however poor he may be must always take rank above an Untouchable, however rich he may be. (Rodrigues 2002, 330)

The problem for Ambedkar was to see the Untouchables become mature (in the Kantian sense of the term) and free of any social, political, or cultural chains. Therefore, unlike Gandhi, he did not share an overwhelming desire to represent Dalits but had the moral courage to support them in their struggle for emancipation. While Gandhi was looking beyond modernity to the assets of the 'village republic', Ambedkar was trying to implement the ideals of liberty, equality, and fraternity of the French Revolution and transform the Indian political society even more deeply by broadening the separation between the temporal and the spiritual. As a result, the freedom that Ambedkar advocated

was not only that of Indians from British rule but also the freedom of the Untouchables from Hindu rule. Indeed, neither
Gandhi nor Nehru did conceive of freedom in these terms: they
did not imagine that the Untouchables needed to be defended
against their own fellow Indians. Moreover, Ambedkar wanted to
end any form of continuity between the Hindu spiritual world
(where right and wrong are decided according to pre-established
laws) and the Hindu temporal world (where the persecution of
Dalits could be enforced because Fundamental Rights were not
practised horizontally). His quest for social justice in the new-
born Indian democracy was also the pursuit of common reason,
which simply meant that the Untouchables could participate
freely and equally in the Indian public debate. In this respect,
however, Ambedkar knew that India still had a long way to go
before achieving its ideal of democracy. Therefore, it would not
be an exaggeration to say that without the heretical Indian there
would be no Indian democracy, and without Indian democracy
there would be no heretical Indian.

# 5

## THE ART OF ANTI-CONFORMISM

All democracies are compelled to create and adopt norms which regulate the behaviours and beliefs of their citizens. However, it would be wrong to believe that a system of government on the whole, because it is democratically elected, has the will and the wish to secure more liberty, more equality, and more social justice to its members. Failure to create new laws or to disobey the existing unjust laws entails the continuance of social evils that endure in democracies. Hence, a democratic society which fails to accept the necessity of heretical personalities cannot remain democratic for long. B.R. Ambedkar was well aware of this fact, but he also knew that his moral capital as a leader with an egalitarian vision did not provide him with sufficient legitimacy to call into question laws of the Hindu religion and those of a temporal Hindu state or society. To his honour, Ambedkar stood all alone in his rejection of unjust laws and regulations in both pre- and post-Independence India. As Aishwary Kumar points out,

> In Ambedkar's thought and writing, neither the radical mobilization of belief nor his resistance against ecclesiastical authority,

neither his defacement and sacrifice of the gods nor the end-
less fascination with divinity's transcendental and imperishable
being, remain wholly separable. Nor above all, can they be easily
extricated from his attempt to craft a new political imagination, a
timeless (if not immortal) republic on which authentic freedom-
the freedom of equals-might be grounded. (Kumar 2015, 32)

What appears clear is that though Ambedkar's understanding of
freedom and democracy is republican in its essence, he refuses
at any rate, like Gandhi, to part with the paradoxes of such a
democracy. In *Caste, Class and Democracy*, he notoriously dis-
cusses the egalitarian essence of democracy beyond universal
adult suffrage.

> Western writers on democracy believe that what is necessary
> for the realization of the ideal of democracy, namely, govern-
> ment by the people, of the people and for the people, is the
> establishment of universal adult suffrage. Other means have
> been suggested such as recall, plebiscite and short parliaments
> and in some countries they have been brought into operation.
> But in a majority of countries nothing more than adult suf-
> frage is deemed to be necessary. I have no hesitation in saying
> that both these notions are fallacious and grossly misleading. If
> democracy and self-government have failed everywhere, it is
> largely due to these wrong notions. ... It may be granted that
> adult suffrage can produce government of the people in the
> logical sense of the phrase, i.e. in contrast to the government
> of a king. But it cannot by itself be said to bring about a demo-
> cratic government, in the sense of government by the people
> and for the people. (Rodrigues 2002, 133)

Applying John Dewey's vision of democracy as 'a way of
life', Ambedkar was very cautious about liberal democracy's

majoritarian stimulus and was more in favour of what Dewey called a 'democratic community'. One is immediately reminded of those memorable pages in Dewey's 'Democracy and Education': 'A democracy, is more than a form of government; it is primarily a mode of associated living, of conjoint communicated experience' (Dewey 1980, 93). In his critique of the Indian society, Ambedkar, therefore, would turn to Dewey as a generative source of democratic thinking. It is not surprising to find many reference to Dewey's work on individualism, democracy, and education in the writings of Ambedkar. '*Annihilation of Caste*' itself ends with a melancholic flourish, its closing pages recounting mournfully what Dewey had called in Individualism Old and New the "tragedy of the lost individual"' (Kumar 2015, 39). As such, the political grammar used by Ambedkar in 'Annihilation of Caste', as in his other writings, bears the Deweyian perception of democracy as a mode of education for the masses and a civic experiment. Dewey was quite aware of the crisis which had affected the American democracy. That is why he believed that democratic habits needed to be changed in order to regulate the fragility of the democratic order. Moreover, Dewey considered democracy as a way of learning and practising the political. To this effect, Dewey developed the idea of democracy as a civic experimentation. Such an approach denotes the education of individual citizens and the democratization of their freedoms. For Dewey, thus, to become democratic a society should help its citizens to become enlightened and provide a readjustment of its social, political, and cultural institutions in relation to the process of this enlightenment. Ambedkar's relentless critique of Hinduism and the advocacy of the 'annihilation of caste' (the title of a polemical pamphlet, the text of an undelivered lecture) diagnosed the elements of inequality in Indian social structures while insisting on the process of rebuilding a political community in India free from the ancient conditions of hierarchy and exploitation.

Ambedkar's groundbreaking text 'Annihilation of Caste' (1939) remains, after 80 years, a highly heretic text. Though never delivered, it was published and immediately confronted and contradicted by grand figures of the Indian Independence movement such as Mahatma Gandhi. Unlike Gandhi, who supported the dharma of *varnashrama* and believed that 'the vast organisation of caste answered not only the religious wants of the community, but it answered too its political needs' (Gandhi 1965, 160–1), Ambedkar was deeply concerned with the social and mental aspects of such an institutionalized injustice. In 'Annihilation of Caste' he wrote:

> It is no use seeking refuge in quibbles. It is no use telling people that the Shastras do not say what they are believed to say, if they are grammatically read or logically interpreted. What matters is how the Shastras have been understood by the people. You must take the stand that Buddha took. You must take the stand which Guru Nanak took. You must not only discard the Shastras, you must deny their authority, as did Buddha and Nanak. You must have courage to tell the Hindus that what is wrong with them is their religion—the religion which has produced in them this notion of the sacredness of Caste. Will you show that courage? (Rodrigues 2002, 291)

As we can see, Ambedkar's heretic strategy of emancipation for the Untouchables went hand in hand with his promotion of a break with the sacredness of Hinduism. His analysis of the caste system was accompanied by an open rejection of an electoral system based on territorial constituencies and the refusal of being subjected to the politically dominant sections of the Hindu society. But Ambedkar's radical and straightforward criticism of the caste system put him in an open controversy with Mahatma Gandhi. Though Ambedkar admitted that Gandhi had challenged untouchability in his politics of Swaraj, he believed that Gandhi's efforts were slow and insufficient. As Christophe Jaffrelot says,

> For Ambedkar, it was impossible to convert the caste system into Chaturvarnya simply by reducing the divisions of four thousand castes within four *varnas* based on individualistic values, because the high castes would never admit merit as the ultimate determinant of social status. Besides, such a transformation implied that one should first destroy the caste system. But, supposing that the transformation of a caste system into a system of *varnas*, found on merit, was practicable, the social functions traditionally associated with various *varnas* would continue to create problems because, for example, intellectual activities would remain the monopoly of Brahmins, whereas the Shudras would continue to work the land and to serve the upper orders. Even if membership of a *varna* is not hereditary in this scheme of things, such specialisation would prove a major obstacle to social mobility. (2005, 72)

It is well known that both Mahatma Gandhi and Dr Ambedkar opposed untouchability and criticized caste. Most Gandhian and Ambedkarite scholars also agree together that while Gandhi criticized untouchability, he defended *varnavyavastha*. However, the truth is that Gandhi and Ambedkar were much closer to each other than is said and written. Already as early as 1927, Gandhi had pointed out that 'if varnashrama goes to the dogs in the removal of Untouchability, I shall not shed a tear' (Gandhi 1969, 'Young India, November 24, 1927', 522–3). Again, returning to the theme of varnas in May 1946, he underlined a yet stronger position:

> I myself have become a harijan by choice. ... A harijan by birth may repudiate his varna but how can I who have become a harijan by choice? I have not hesitated to suggest to caste Hindus that today they have all to become ati-shudras, if the canker of caste feeling is to be eradicated from Hinduism and Hinduism is not to perish from the face of the earth. (Gandhi 1981, 'Speech at Prayer Meeting, May 31, 1946', 247)

A mere critic of Gandhi might see only inconsistency in his attitudes regarding the problem of caste and varna over his lifetime. Though Gandhi was an admirer of the *varnavyavastha*, he believed that there was no social or political hierarchy between castes in the India of his dream. But Ambedkar knew that preaching and fasting against untouchability and the caste system was not enough. According to him, what was needed was not the tolerance of the Untouchables but the dissent of the Dalits. That dissent remains at the heart of Ambedkar's struggle for appearance in the public space; this is what makes his heretical mindset even more relevant in today's Indian society. Unlike Gandhi, who is elevated by many in India and elsewhere to the level of sainthood, B.R. Ambedkar was not a saint. He was a heretic who died in debt, but who promoted justice and dignity for the Dalits in India. He considered equality as a regulating principle of human societies because, for him, injustice was the mother of all social ills. He pointed out: 'You cannot build anything on the foundations of caste. You cannot build up a nation;

you cannot build up a morality. Anything that you will build on the foundations of caste will crack and will never be a whole' (Rodrigues 2002, 287–8).

A social revolution or, more exactly, a revolution of values was what Ambedkar was striving for in the Indian society. With this perspective, he pursued the ideas of self-government and self-development for the Untouchables. He spelt out, in an even stronger tone, the political nature of this self-government. In his second editorial for the Marathi fortnightly *Mooknayak*,

> Ambedkar said, self-government was not something that could be obtained by raising slogans. He said that none of the self-appointed leaders of the people could take credit for beginnings of self-government in India. The measure of self-government that had been granted to the Indians, was more a consequence to the wisdom of the rulers than those clamouring for it. The British had laid the foundations of self-government in India out of love for the principles they propounded. The institutions of local self-government and of provincial and supreme councils had not resulted from the urgings of any advocate who had gone to plead for them. Therefore, no one should forget that this bonnie child of self-government that could be seen in the country owed its existence to the British. (Cited in Gore 1993, 82–3)

Though Ambedkar was well aware of what was due to the Untouchables by right, he exhorted the Untouchables to recognize their strength in confronting the caste Hindus. He wrote:

> The civil right of an individual is not established by a decree. It is an inherent right. ... Therefore we would like to warn the caste Hindus as also our fellow Untouchables that though

Untouchables may be weak in some respects they are not entirely helpless. The caste Hindus should seriously think what would happen to Hindu society if the Untouchables were to declare a boycott of Hinduism and convert themselves to Islam. (Cited in Gore 1993, 94–6)

It is interesting that Ambedkar already had the idea of 'conversion' in mind back in 1920 as a strategy to exit Hinduism and have relations with other groups. Assuredly, he felt that India was a stratified society where the attainment of self-governance was not enough. He was looking for a religious revolution (as in the case of Martin Luther and Reformation) in Hinduism, which could precede a social and political revolution in India. Dr Ambedkar saw a link between the two, because, for him, the existing social order in India (which needed a revolution of values) was the Hindu religious and social order. In order to prove his point, Dr Ambedkar quoted Hindu texts and pointed to 'varna' as the unit of Hindu society and the foundation of the existing Indian social order. Given this, Ambedkar's first heretic move was to define religion as 'the propounding of an ideal scheme of divine governance, the aim and object of which is to make the social order in which men live a moral order' (cited in Gore 1993, 231).

Ambedkar did not believe in a general philosophy of religion, since each religion had its own philosophy according to him. However, he was aware of the fact that every religion deals with what is right and what is wrong. So, the whole idea of revolution in religion was about a revolution in values. As he underlines, the revolution in religion was not 'merely a revolution in the religious organisation of society, resulting in shifting of the focus—from society to the individual, it was a revolution in norms' (cited in Gore 1993, 233). It is interesting that Ambedkar never put into question the perennial human need for religion. What interested him was to be able to weaken the role of religion in the Indian society as a social force, and also to show that the norms of a modern society, such as post-Revolution France, were equality, liberty, and fraternity. Ambedkar believed that the French Revolution set the essentials of a non-hierarchical order. He writes: 'If you ask me, my ideal would be a society based on *Liberty, Equality and Fraternity*. And why not? What objection can there be to fraternity? I cannot imagine any' (Rodrigues 2002, 276).

Moreover, Ambedkar developed at different occasions the three principles of liberty, equality, and fraternity. For example, in his 'Annihilation of Caste', he suggested these three principles as the basis for Hinduism. 'Whether you do that or you do not, you must give a new doctrinal basis to your religion— a basis that will be in consonance with Liberty, Equality and Fraternity, in short, with Democracy' (Rodrigues 2002, 301). We can also find a clear vision of the principles of the French Revolution in Ambedkar's essay entitled 'Buddha or Karl Marx', where he refers to these three principles as spiritual outcomes. He affirms:

Man must grow materially as well as spiritually. Society has been aiming to lay a new foundation was summarised by the French Revolution in three words, Fraternity, Liberty and Equality. The French Revolution was welcomed because of this slogan. It failed to produce equality. We welcome the Russian Revolution because it aims to produce equality. But it cannot be too much emphasised that in producing equality society cannot afford to sacrifice fraternity or liberty. Equality will be of no value without fraternity or liberty. It seems that the three can coexist only if one follows the way of the Buddha. Communism can give one but not all. (Rodrigues 2002, 189)

Notice that Ambedkar salutes the Russian Revolution but remains critical of it. He refuses to admit the historical necessity of the proletariat's dictatorship. Furthermore, Ambedkar is not a typical secularist *à la française* (in a French way), putting the French *laïcité* (secularism) ahead of the spiritual wisdom that he finds in Buddhism. That is why he blames the Russian communists for not keeping an eye on the communist doctrine of the Buddha. Ambedkar affirms:

> The Russians do not seem to be paying any attention to Buddhism as an ultimate aid to sustain Communism when force is withdrawn. The Russians are proud of their Communism. But they forget that the wonder of all wonders is that the Buddha established Communism so far as the Sangh was concerned without dictatorship. It may be that it was a communism on a very small scale but it was communism without dictatorship, a miracle which Lenin failed to do. The Buddha's method was different. His method was to change the mind of man: to alter his disposition: so that whatever man does, he does it voluntarily without the use of force or compulsion. His main means to alter the disposition of men was his Dhamma and the constant preaching of his Dhamma. The Buddhas way was not to force people to do what they did not like to do although it was good for them. His way was to alter the disposition of men so that they would do voluntarily what they would not otherwise to do. (Rodrigues 2002, 189)

It seems important to note the political context in which the question of Buddha's 'communism' is posed by Ambedkar, while he constantly refused to delve into questions of God and eschatology. Though Ambedkar preferred Buddhism to Hinduism, he also considered himself as a socialist. He, therefore, considered Communism as the theory of the emancipation of the proletariat. But, for Ambedkar, the lowered castes in India definitely represented the Indian proletariat, which was born of the varna system and was not necessarily the product of any industrial revolution. That is to say, the influence of Marx on Ambedkar is apparent in his views on the emancipation of the workers, but he was undoubtedly not in favour of extinguishing perennial norms and values. To make a strong case for Ambedkar, we need to understand how and why he kept his distance from both liberalism and Marxism while defending a certain idea of democracy. From the discussion so far, it should be clear that Ambedkar's idea of democracy, which was founded on the political and educational principles of John Dewey, put into question the very foundation of the notion of Indian democracy as unity in diversity. Ambedkar offered his own corrective to Indian history, as suggested by Jawaharlal Nehru in his *Discovery of India*.

The main difference was in the relative significance they attached to particular events. Thus, while Nehru was aware that Brahmanism had regained a foothold during the immediate post-Mauryan period and that the Sunga kings had revived the performance of sacrifices, he mentioned this only in passing. For Ambedkar this was a turning point. While Nehru attached importance to the schism that developed in Buddhism and the proliferation of ritual in the Mahayana Buddhist sect and treated them as explanatory causes in the decline of Buddhism, Ambedkar regarded these as only a development consequential

on the active persecution of Buddhism by the Brahmans, under
royal patronage. (Gore 1993, 311)

Since Ambedkar, in the manner of Dewey, considered democracy as a form of society, he was not really concerned by the
Nehruvian idea of 'unity'. On the contrary, what was central to
Ambedkar's idea of democracy was the concept of 'equal fellow-
ship'. He emphasized:

> It may not be necessary for a democratic society to be marked by
> unity, by community of purpose, by loyalty to public ends and
> by mutuality of sympathy. But it does unmistakably involve two
> things. The first is an attitude of mind, an attitude of respect and
> equality towards their fellows. The second is a social organization
> free from rigid social barriers. (Ambedkar 1979, 'Ranade, Gandhi
> and Jinnah', 222)

What sense can we make of Ambedkar's heretic construct
of the public sphere? Let us remember that Ambedkar develops the idea of heresy through the two questions of: 'by what
right?' and 'through what means?' This means that the exercise
of heresy can take place precisely in relation to the assertions of
a Hindu state over the Untouchables. After all, for Ambedkar,
what should be developed and displayed as heretical imperative
is precisely the operation that asks by what right and through
what means are certain religious or political dogmas accepted
at a pre-critical stage. As a result, for Ambedkar, heresy is not
to be understood as a simple act of questioning, which happens
exclusively at a precise time and a precise place. To ask what is
heresy and what is heretical about Ambedkar is effectively to
show that heresy is something that could and should take place
with the question of questioning. The core idea of Ambedkar's
heretic philosophy is his unfaltering and unflinching conviction

that it is no longer possible to have a social organization of justice without heresy. In other words, according to Ambedkar, democracy, to be worthy of its concept and name, must be defined and organized so that every citizen can bring forward his heretical questioning into the public realm. At stake here, however, is the question of whether we can continue to think about heresy, from an Ambedkarian perspective, as something more than simple controversy or nay-saying. Is it right to be burned at the stake for one's belief against all forms of dogmatism and orthodoxy. Heresy, it turns out, is an immensely courageous mode of thinking and questioning which always remains fragmentary and marginalized at the expense of larger truths. At that point, it may well be that a heretic character such as Ambedkar continues to offer us meaningful questions while sheltering the possibilities of questions yet to be asked. Great works of heresy remain, as in the case of Ambedkar, as does our heretical need to read them and find a way to turn the page.

# 6

# AMBEDKAR'S PHILOSOPHY
# OF HERESY

Ambedkar was one of the most innovative and insightful political thinkers of the last century, but a thinker, unfortunately, largely ignored by the rest of the world. Practically everybody around the globe knows the name of Mahatma Gandhi, but many university students and their instructors have never heard of Bhimrao Ramji Ambedkar. Yet, Ambedkar was a multidimensional heretic. He was a lawyer who knew how to disobey unjust laws, a constitutionalist who had the talent to draft a controversial constitution, and a political practitioner who practised politics with the people and not with the political elite. As such, Ambedkar's political philosophy was born of a reflection on his own political experience as a Dalit. In particular, his thinking about Indian democracy is not a new tryout of abstract ideas, but rather an attempt to evoke an equitable and fraternal experience of democracy. More specifically, it is a lived experience of the dissolution of the Hindu markers of identity that characterize the Indian society. The Ambedkarian struggle for the humanization of the downtrodden in the Indian society was a supreme act of heresy as a sign of breakdown with regard to human relations in the public sphere. Ambedkar's heretical act was the proper answer to the unstable pivotal situation which continues to tear apart Indian social life. As in all pivotal situations, Ambedkar came across a critical juncture regarding the problem of caste in the Indian society and made a courageous choice (αἵρεσις) as the appropriate way forward. Today, more than 60 years after Dr Ambedkar's death, many Indians still need this courage to annihilate the mental ghettos of casteism. But this cannot be achieved, as Arundhati Roy puts it correctly, 'unless we read Babasaheb Ambedkar. If not inside our classrooms, then outside them. Until then we will remain what he called the "sick men" and women of Hinduism, who seem to have no desire to get well' (Roy 2019, 124).

Ambedkar's big heretic choice was his conversion to Buddhism on 11 October 1956. This conversion was, in fact, the most countering example of his heresy. In this regard, it has been an integral part of his philosophical and political struggle against the Indian apartheid. Dr Ambedkar did not convert to Buddhism in order to escape the caste system. He converted in order to fight the caste mentality. This is evident from his statement at the Mahad Conference: 'We want equal rights in society. We will achieve them as far as possible while remaining within the Hindu fold or, if necessary, by kicking away this worthless Hindu identity. And if it becomes necessary for us to give up Hinduism it would no longer be necessary for us to bother about temples' (cited in Gore 1993, 91). This was not the first time that Ambedkar had considered the possibility of the Untouchables exiting Hinduism. He had already expressed his desire to abandon Hinduism in 1927. He made his next important move regarding conversion in October 1935 at a meeting on Depressed Classes in Yeola. At this meeting, he went on to underline the failure of his attempts to ensure that the Untouchables be allowed to enter temples. He asserted:

> The disabilities we have suffered and the indignities we had to put up with, were the result of our being the members of the Hindu Community. Will it not be better for us to leave that fold and embrace a new faith that would give us equal status, a secure position and rightful treatment? I advise you to severe your connection with Hinduism and to embrace any other religion. But, in doing so be careful in choosing the new faith and see that equality in treatment, status and opportunities will be guaranteed to you unreservedly. Unfortunately for me I was born a Hindu Untouchable. It was beyond my power to prevent that, but I declare that it is within my power to refuse to live under ignoble and humiliating conditions. I solemnly assure you that I will not die a Hindu. (Cited in Narake 2003, 94–5)

For Ambedkar, conversion was not only a means of civil disobedience but also a path to gain dignity and self-respect. He weighed the merits of Buddhism, as an Indian religion, against the merits of Hinduism and finally resolved to embrace Buddhism. Perhaps this is the main reason why Dr Ambedkar dismissed the idea of converting to Islam or Christianity, both Abrahamic religions, or Sikhism, a faith particular to Punjab. Comparing these three religions, he declared:

> Islam seems to give the Depressed Classes all that they need. Financially the resources behind Islam are boundless. Socially the Mohammedans are spread all over India. ... Politically, the Depressed Classes will get all rights, which the Mohammedans are entitled to ... Christianity seems equally attractive. If Indian

Christians are too small numerically to provide the financial resources necessary for the conversion of the Depressed Classes, the Christian countries such as America and England will pour immense resources if the Depressed Classes show their readiness to embrace Christianity. ... Sikhism has few attractions. Being a small community of 40 lakhs, the Sikhs cannot provide the finance. ... They are confined to the Punjab, and as for the majority of the Depressed Classes the Sikhs can give them no social support. Politically, Sikhism is at a positive disadvantage as compared with Islam or Christianity. Outside Punjab, Sikhs are not recognized for special representation in the Legislature and in the services. (Jafferlot 2005, 121–2)

By refusing to convert to Islam and Christianity, Ambedkar was keeping his distance from the two discourses of 'denationalization' and 'separation'. But there was another reason for this: by converting to Buddhism, Ambedkar and the Untouchables would not be implicated in any foreign 'conspiracies' or 'extra-Indian political plans'. According to Christophe Jaffrelot in his brilliant study in *Dr. Ambedkar and Untouchability*:

Arab press expressed its interest in Ambedkar's plans [concerning conversion] while the vice-chancellor of Al-Azhar University in Cairo—which raised funds to facilitate a possible mass conversion—explained that it was not necessary to be circumcised or to wear the veil to become a Muslim. He even sent a delegation to India in December 1936. From October 1935, Maulana Mohammed Irfan, a representative of India's Khilafat Central Committee, assured Ambedkar that Islam was an egalitarian religion and conversion would allow him to become a leader of India's largest minority. The same month, Maulana Ahmed Sa'id, the head of the Indian Association of Ulemas, sent him a similar message. The Muslims of Punjab entrusted a

new convert-Kanhiya Lal Gauba-, a member of the Legistaive
Assembly, to persuade Ambedkar to opt for Islam. Many
ulemas, in particular in the Muslim princely states, appealed to
Untouchables with the same objective. (2005, 124)

In August 1936, Ambedkar abandoned the prospect of
Untouchables converting to any of the three mentioned religions.
The reason was simple: the idea of exiting the Hindu system of
castes was a political choice for him, not a religious one. This is
why he insisted on the 'egalitarian' creed of Buddhism. By converting the Untouchables to another religion (that is, Buddhism)
Ambedkar was not hoping that they would gain wealth. Instead,
his intention was to empower them in a process of social transformation. Ambedkar considered conversion as important to the
Untouchables as Swaraj was to India. According to him, both
had freedom as the final end.

As we can see, for Ambedkar conversion was a great struggle
for choice and autonomy. He saw the moral legitimacy and
political value of conversion in its heretic feature of gaining
freedom. Far from treating freedom as a mere word, he considered it as providing power of having a dissident voice. He
saw a direct link between the conversion of the Untouchables
and their social freedom. But the most central and far-reaching
question that Ambedkar tried to answer through the emancipative strategy of conversion was: Who will we be and what shall
be our path? Ambedkar understood conversion in its proper
sense as deriving from the Latin root word *conversio*, which
means a turning round, revolving, and revolution. But originally,
*conversio* is an act of change, alteration, and subversion. We can
understand hereby the heretic nature of Ambedkar's conversion
to Buddhism. His deep desire to embrace Buddhism was not

necessarily to follow a new sense of the sacred but to abandon and renounce Hinduism. His final goal was the political representation of the Untouchables in Indian society. As a rationalist who was at war with the evils of blind prejudice and limitations of religious dogmas, Ambedkar could not have been at peace with any established religious systems. For him, the Buddha was also a heretic in Hinduism as was Jesus in Judaism. However, the Buddha, more than being a prophet, was a man who was in rebellion against Hindu orthodoxy.

Ambedkar did not believe in the philosophy of reincarnation or that the Buddha was an incarnation of Vishnu. Thus, it would be more correct to say that he was attracted more by Buddhist ethics than by Buddhist theology. Another point to notice here is that Ambedkar's heretic act of conversion to Buddhism was also a republican gesture of highlighting the egalitarian principle that he found in the French Revolution. As such, the equality of human beings as a key principle in Buddhism was considered by him as a strong alternative to the authoritarian social hierarchy of Hinduism. Undoubtedly, his interest in Buddhism is quite compatible with the Kantian idea of Enlightenment as the exit of humanity from its self-incurred immaturity. According to him, where the goal of Buddhism is to assist human beings to operate in the open, Hinduism keeps them imprisoned in the dark. In his interpretation of Buddhism, Ambedkar was attracted by its transparent, lucid, and honest nature. For him, Dhamma was a philosophy of understanding human beings and the world. As he puts it himself,

> The Buddha's method was different. His method was to change the mind of man: to alter his disposition: so that whatever man does, he does it voluntarily without the use of force or

compulsion. His main means to alter the disposition of men was his Dhamma and the constant preaching of his Dhamma. The Buddhas way was not to force people to do what they did not like to do although it was good for them. His way was to alter the disposition of men so that they would do voluntarily what they would not otherwise to do. (Rodrigues 2002, 189)

This egalitarianism of the Buddha represented for Ambedkar the core of the values that he tried to include in what he called 'constitutional morality'. Developing this idea in the Constituent Assembly on 4 November 1948, he said: 'Constitutional morality is not a natural sentiment. It has to be cultivated. We must realise that our people have yet to learn it. Democracy in India is only a top dressing on an Indian soil which is essentially undemocratic' (Das 2010, 175). Ambedkar thought of the Indian Constitution as a learning process for the Indian people. And yet, his mentality was far more radical than that of the Indian Constitution. He was thinking of repeating in India what the French revolutionaries had done in France in 1789 and 1791.

For Ambedkar, participating in the making of the Indian Constitution was a form of moral commitment to the principles of justice, equality, and liberty. If anything, Ambedkar's interventions in the debates of the Constituent Assembly in the late 1940s prepared the terrain for his turbulent and dissident interventions as the law minister and as the chief chairman of the Drafting Committee of the Indian Constitution. Ambedkar was not necessarily on the same page as his colleagues of the Drafting Committee. His active participation in all the meetings was a sign of his enthusiasm to integrate the two ideas of human dignity and social equality into the Indian Constitution. For him, the best way to insert an anti-discrimination law in the Indian

Constitution, thus, was not only by asking for equality but also by providing a remedy for inequality. 'But the Constitution did not provide for separate electorates in the case of either the scheduled castes or the religious minorities. Nor did the idea that Ambedkar had mooted in his *States and Minorities*, of a cabinet composed of persons elected by different communities, find any support in the assembly' (Gore 1993, 185). This does not mean that Ambedkar's participation in drafting the Indian Constitution was guided only by his interest in the future of the Untouchables. Quite the contrary, Ambedkar was concerned with the inegalitarian essence of the Indian caste-based society and believed, as a result, that Indian democracy could not and would not survive without social democracy. Referring to 26 January 1950, the day the Constitution was adopted in the Constituent Assembly, he underlined: 'We are going to enter into a life of contradictions. In politics we will have equality and in social and economic life we will have inequality. ... We must remove this contradiction at the earliest possible moment or else those who suffer from inequality will blow up the structure of political democracy which this Assembly has so laboriously built up' (cited in Gore 1993, 187).

Unlike Gandhi, Nehru, Patel, and Maulana Azad, for Ambedkar, there was no such thing as an Indian nation as long as India remained a caste-based society. While stoutly defending the Constitution, Ambedkar came to this idea of an 'unachieved' Indian nation. He affirmed,

> I am of opinion that in believing we are a nation, we are cherishing a great illusion. How can people divided into several thousands of castes be a nation? The sooner we realise that we are not as yet a nation in the social and psychological sense of the word,

the better for us. For then only we shall realise the necessity of becoming a nation and seriously think of ways and means of realising the goal. (Gore 1993, 187)

With this in mind, Ambedkar made it clear to his contemporaries that even in an independent India, the Untouchables remained socially excluded and morally unequal. Consequently, he did not consider himself as the 'father' or the 'architect' of the Indian Constitution. It is in this relation that he announced in 1953 that he was ready to burn out this document. 'Sir, my friends tell me that I made the Constitution,' wrote Ambedkar only few days after the adoption of the Indian Constitution, 'but I am quite prepared to say that I shall be the first person to burn it out' (Keer 1971 [1954], 499). It is undeniable that there is something radically heretic about Ambedkar's mode of thinking here. This heretic thought has troubled modern Indian society since its inception. However, it also has an emancipatory virtue, asking Indian citizens to look beyond their Constitution and their state laws. As a matter of fact, the dissident wholeness of Ambedkar's oeuvre is heretic in nature. His refusal to dissociate the culture of civic dissidence from the question of 'constitutional morality' takes him beyond ordinary legalistic thinking and opens new dimensions of republican sovereignty which does not exclude the weakest and the most vulnerable. According to Ambedkar,

> While everybody recognizes the necessity of diffusion of constitutional morality for the peaceful working of the democratic constitution, there are two things interconnected with it which are not, unfortunately, generally recognized. One is that the form of administration must be appropriate to and in the same sense as the form of the Constitution. The other is that it is perfectly

possible to pervert the Constitution, without changing its form by merely changing its form of administration and to make it inconsistent and opposed to the spirit of the Constitution. ('Motion on the Draft Constitution', 4 November 1948, cited in Kumar 2015, 260)

Therefore, from Ambedkar's point of view, the lesser the intervention of the Indian state is in the autonomous actions of its citizens, the stronger would be the Indian nation's tradition of constitutional morality.

Ambedkar was well aware of the fact that India had never been possessed with any manner of a democratic tradition in the modern sense of the term. Therefore, to insert a democratic spirit into the Indian society and heal the damages wrought by centuries of inequality and injustice was a difficult task. Maybe that is why he saluted Mahatma Gandhi's criticism of social injustice in India, but found it insufficient. On the occasion of a conference on the Depressed Classes, he affirmed: 'Before Mahatma Gandhi, no politician in this country maintained that it is necessary to remove social injustice here in order to do away with tension and conflict, and that every Indian should consider it his sacred duty to do so' (cited in Pantham 2009, 186–7). However, as we have shown previously, Ambedkar considered Gandhi as a thinker and practitioner who did not want to take radical measures concerning the caste system, for Gandhi did not insist on the removal of Untouchability as much as he insisted on the propagation of Hindu–Muslim unity. This, undoubtedly, would not have been the case if Mahatma Gandhi was not assassinated on 30 January 1948. It should also be added that Gandhi was the first Indian politician to link the issue of Swaraj with that of Untouchability. But Ambedkar was too much of a heretic for the disobedient Indian that Gandhi was. By early 1930s, his faith in the Congress Party and the bureaucratic action for Independence had been eroded and, therefore, he favored a political strategy that was more citizen based. Gandhi and many others believed that Ambedkar's heretic critique of Hinduism would create a lot of trouble in the Indian society. They were right, but this was exactly what Ambedkar was looking for. His critique of Hinduism, caste-based relations, the Indian Constitution, and so on, was a wake-up call for pre- and post-Independence India. For Ambedkar, social justice, not only Swaraj, was the fundamental law of the Indian society. He fought for social justice throughout his career. Equal citizenship, for Ambedkar, was the liberating principle of the Untouchables in particular and the Indian society in general. The truth is that he was not comfortable with many aspects of the Indian tradition. He, therefore, refrained from reframing it, as Gandhi and Tagore did. He decided to reject it. In doing so, Ambedkar remained faithful to his heretical self and to his heretical action. Assuredly, anyone who has no taste for heresy finds it extremely difficult to understand the life and works of Babasaheb Ambedkar in a manner which would make it a consistent whole. Thus, in a final analysis, Ambedkar remains our contemporary, neither because he has joined posthumously the mainstream of the Indian nationalist narrative, nor because the new sociopolitical arrangement of the Indian society by the Hindutva has been able to dismiss and discard the message of Ambedkar, but, more importantly, because Ambedkar's writings are the ideas whose time has come. No society can resist an idea whose time has come. No society can resist heretics, that is why they are burned at the stake. This appears to be a tragic but inevitable law of history. Let us not forget, however, that

Victor Hugo, Herbert Spencer, and Henrik Ibsen raised a statue in the honour of Giordano Bruno in Rome's Campo de' Fiori. Nearly 420 years after Bruno was burned naked at the stake by the Inquisition, on the anniversary of his execution, various individuals gather at his monument every year and pay tribute to a man who was accused of heresy. Ironically, the inscription at the base of his statue reads: 'To Bruno, from the generation that he foresaw.' This generation is yet to arrive in India. This is a generation which will have the courage to speak up beyond castes, religious dogmas, traditions, and mental ghettos. This will be a generation of individuals who will attempt to develop their singularity in a reflected manner, the same way Ambedkar did.

# CONCLUSION
## Being Heretic Today

Humanity will not be enslaved so long as it continues to produce heretics. Though it is true that the world today is short in supply of heretics, yet heresy remains a philosophical horizon of hope for all those who continue to believe in its significance and the possibility of a revolution of values. Heretics continue to remind us of the inherent fragility of human existence and the frailty of the human political condition, while serving as a reference point for all future critiques of conformity and mediocrity in our world. The act of heresy, which ultimately cost Giordano Bruno as well as other heretics their lives, is not a random choice. An entire host of processes are involved in the act of heresy, which, as we saw all through this book, turn it into a heroic act. As a matter of fact, heresy establishes the supremacy of a thinking, reflective, and critical human being who dares not only to speak back to power, over the arbitrary acts of tyrants, but also to move against the tide. This is what dissent is about and we all know that there is an urgent need to reiterate the right to dissent in the current

climate of populism and fanaticism which promotes mediocrity and thoughtlessness.

In the absence of heretics, those who can make us believe
in lies can make us commit murders and mass killings. There
is, therefore, more to heresy. It is closely connected to justice.
Justice is meaningless without the heretic questioning of the
unjust and the unthought. The course of thinking and questioning is a necessary part of the heretical imperative. And some-
times, if not always, the heretical imperative to question and
to dissent represents the acme of freedom. When an individual
realizes her/his heretical move through critical reflection and
critique of power, she/he exercises dissent. Thus, for the political
philosopher, heresy is the highest form of dissent. The questioning and dissenting heretic has to be prepared to live a life of
marginality, as many heretics did, and ultimately die because
she/he disturbed conformity and challenged the contemptible
mediocrities of complacency.

There can exist no phenomenological process of civilization-
making without a strong sense of heresy. However, the claim
that heretical imperative rests on the authority of tradition
in general denies the possibility of critical self-reflection and
its ability to break with the dogmatic elements in every tradition of thought, which works against any effort of medita-
tive thinking. As such, what can make the state of heretical
thinking authentic is neither the simple work of rationality, nor
an empathetic sharing of life with others, but an acid test of
the human existential situation in our century. As a matter of
fact, our humanity is measured not only by our belonging to
a culture but also by our critical attitude towards it. Culture,
is not, as Matthew Arnold discussed, simply 'the best that has

been thought and said in the world' (cited in Storey 1997, 14).
Culture is what gives humans the critical capacity to be heretics. The relevant question, therefore, does not concern why
there are no heretics, but what do heretics do with their heresy
if they exist in our world. In other words, the true question is
whether we are at a point in history when humanity has lost
its faith in heretics or it is still capable of forging new forms of
heretical thinking.

We live in a time of widespread relativism, conformism,
and complacency, which has created an attitude of ethical
passivity, a flattering mode of being, and a mood of 'anything
goes' for the new generation. It is also a time that is witness-
ing widespread public scepticism about the critical role of
thinking. Thus, the claim that heresy is a liberating activity is
likely to be met with cynicism and derision of the masses. As a
result, it would be hard not to see that the political incompe-
tence and ethical ineptitude of our contemporary civilization
has slammed the door in the face of what we can call 'living
with heretics'. This is the basic existential starting point of an
ethical commitment to the questioning of public good. This
moral courage to take responsibility is also the courage to raise
philosophical questions about the destiny of our democracies.
It goes without saying that democracy without its complement
of the heretical courage to ask heretical questions falls short of
being a democracy. Heresy is a concept that has not only been
poorly understood but also been intensely misused. This dually
unfortunate condition of heresy brings to the forefront of all
philosophical and political discussions the idea that heresy is
a struggle for freedom, as an important part of being free is

thinking heretically. As we can see, the problem of freedom arises within every consideration of the nature of heretical questioning itself. If the point of the nature of heretical questioning is to consider the concept of freedom, so that human beings can conform to it, some account must be given of how our civilization could have strayed from that questioning in the first place and how it might be possible to return.

It is the political task of heresy to resist the very idea of a conformist and unquestionable theory of politics. To demand that the political organization of a society should be founded on a non-dissenting attitude is, therefore, to declare politics non-thinkable and to put an end to the freedom of thinking otherwise and of thinking anew. In other words, a democratic society cannot exist without heretical questioning or, to say it more clearly, without a heretical questioning of the nature of democracy. There is little point in talking and writing about heresy without having to reflect on the nature of heresy itself. This is why the function of the heretic, as a person whose mind watches the mediocrities and injustices of the world, should be maintained, even if the concept of heresy has lost its political strength today. Let us not forget that the main task of heretics is not to create iron cages of ignorance and stupidity but to destroy them. Heretics, thus, still have a lot to contribute to the thoughtfulness of thinking. They will certainly be useful to human societies as long as humans continue to believe that heresy is not a futile word and action. In a way, the critical task of heretics today is with regard to the struggle between thinking and what has become unquestionable in our political and cultural institutions. Whatever the

price may be that heretics pay for their empty hands in the
battle against these thoughtless and servant-making institutions, we can always hope that they continue to hit the targets
that no one else can see or wants to see. After all, the task of
heretics is to think and change what nobody wants to think
about or change.

# BIBLIOGRAPHY

Abelsen, Peter. 1966. 'Irony and Purity: Mishima'. *Modern Asian Studies* 30, no. 3: 651–79.

Ahir, D.C. 1990. *The Legacy of Dr. Ambedkar*. New Delhi: B.R. Publishing Corporation.

———. 1997. *Dr. Ambedkar on the British Raj*. Delhi: Blumoon Books.

Aloysius, G. 2017. 'Ambedkar's Political Nationalism'. In *Contemporary Relevance of Ambedkar's Thoughts*, edited by Avatthi Ramaiah, Chapter 6. New Delhi: Rawat Publications.

Ambedkar, B.R. 1979. *Dr. Babasaheb Ambedkar: Writings and Speeches*, volume 1, edited by V. Moon. Bombay: Education Department, Government of Maharashtra.

———. 1987. *Dr. Babasaheb Ambedkar: Writings and Speeches*, volumes 3 and 4, edited by V. Moon. Bombay: Education Department, Government of Maharashtra.

———. 1995. *Annihilation of Castes*. Jalandhar: Bheem Patrika Publications.

———. 2017. 'A Nation Calling for a Home'. *Coldnoon: International Journal of Travel Writing and Travelling Cultures*. Available at https://coldnoon.com/magazine/classics/a-nation-calling-for-a-home/. Last accessed on 14 August 2020.

Arendt, Hannah. 1958a. *The Human Condition*. Chicago: University of Chicago Press.

———. 1958b. *The Origins of Totalitarianism*. New York: World Publishing.

Ashok, D.S. 1997. *Dr. B.R. Ambedkar's Thoughts and Role in the Nation Building*. Mathura, UP: Prabhat Printing Press.

Balachandran, Mira. 2009. *Quotation for All Occasions*. Chennai: Emerald Publishers.

Batia, K.L., O.M. Hari, and R. Chowdhary. 1993. *Social Justice of Dr. B.R. Ambedkar*. New Delhi: Deep and Deep Publications.

Bonefeld, Werner. 2017. *The Strong State and the Free Economy*. Maryland: Rowman & Littlefield.

Brown, Harold O.J. 2018. *Heresy and Orthodoxy in the History of the Church*. Peabody, Massachusetts: Hendrickson Publishers.

Camus, Albert. 1948. *The Plague*. London: Penguin Books.

———. 1955. *The Myth of Sisyphus and Other Essays*. New York: Vintage Books.

———. 1956. *The Rebel: An Essay on Man in Revolt*. New York: Vintage Books.

———. 1958. 'Camus at Stockholm: The Acceptance of the Nobel Prize', translated by Justin O'Brien. *Atlantic Monthly* 201 (May): 33–4.

———. 1963. *Notebooks 1935–1942*. New York: Alfred A. Knopf.

———. 1968. 'The New Mediterranean Culture'. In *Lyrical and Critical Essays*, 189–99. New York: Vintage Books.

———. 1995a. 'Bread and Freedom'. In *Resistance Rebellion, and Death*, 87–97. New York: Vintage Books.

———. 1995b. 'Create Dangerously'. In *Resistance Rebellion, and Death*, 249–72. New York: Vintage Books.

———. 1995c. 'Letters to a German Friend' In *Resistance Rebellion, and Death*, 1–33. New York: Vintage Books.

———. 2008. *Neither Victims nor Executioners: An Ethic Superior to Murder*. New York: Wipf & Stock.

Castoriadis, Cornelius. 1987. *The Imaginary Institution of Society*, translated by Kathleen Blamey. Cambridge: Polity Press.

———. 1991. *Philosophy Politics Autonomy: Essays in Political Philosophy.* Oxford: Oxford University Press.

Das, Bhagawan. 2010. *Thus Spoke Ambedkar*, Volume 1: *A Stake in the Nation*. New Delhi: Navayana.

Dewey, John. 1980. *The Middle Works: 1899–1924*, Volume 9: *1916*, edited by J.A. Boydston, P. Baysinger, and P. Levine. Carbondale: Southern Illinois University Press.

Dobson, Andrew. 2009. *An Introduction to the Politics and Philosophy of Jose Ortega y Gasset*. Cambridge: Cambridge University Press.

Emerson, Ralph Waldo. 1903. *Essays*. New York: Carleton House.

Gandhi, M.K. 1965. *The Collected Works of Mahatma Gandhi (CWMG)*, volume 15. New Delhi: Publications Division, Government of India.

———. 1969. *The Collected Works of Mahatma Gandhi (CWMG)*, volume 35. New Delhi: Publications Division, Government of India.

———. 1981. *The Collected Works of Mahatma Gandhi (CWMG)*, volume 84. New Delhi: Publications Division, Government of India.

Ghatak, B.K., ed. 1997. *Dr. Ambedkar's Thought*. New Delhi: A.P.H. Publishing Corporation.

Gore, M.S. 1993. *The Social Context of an Ideology: Ambedkar's Political and Social Thought*. New Delhi: Sage Publications.

Grover, V., ed. 1993. *B.R. Ambedkar*. New Delhi: Deep and Deep Publications.

Guru, Gopal, ed. 2011. *Humiliation: Claims and Context*. New Delhi: Oxford University Press.

Havel, Valcav. 1985. 'The Power of the Powerless'. In *The Power of the Powerless: Citizens against the state in central-eastern Europe*, edited by John Keane, 23–96. London: Routledge.

———. 1990. *Disturbing Peace: A Conversation with Karel Hvizdala*. New York: Vintage Books.

Heidegger, Martin. 1976. *What Is Called Thinking?* New York: Harper
    Perennial.

Herndon, Jerry A. 1969. 'St. Paul and Emerson's Self Reliance'. *Americ*
    *an Transcendental Quarterly* 1: 90.

Inose, Naoki, and Hiroaki Sato. 2012. *Persona: A Biography of Yukio*
    *Mishima*. Berkeley, California: Stone Bridge Press.

Jaffrelot, Christophe. 2005. *Dr. Ambedkar and Untouchability: Analyzing*
    *and Fighting Caste*. New York: Columbia University Press.

Jaffrelot, Christophe, and Narendra Kumar, ed. 2018. *Dr. Ambedkar*
    *and Democracy: An Anthology*. New Delhi: Oxford University Press.

Kadam, K.N., ed. 1993. *Dr. Ambedkar: The Emancipator of the Oppressed*.
    Bombay: Popular Prakashan.

Kant, Immanuel. 1991. *The Answer to the Question: What is*
    *Enlightenment?* of the Great Ideas series. London: Penguin Books.

Keer, Dhananjay. 1971 [1954]. *Dr. Ambedkar: Life and Mission*. Bombay:
    Popular Prakashan.

Kieckhefer, Richard. 1979. *Repression of Heresy in Medieval Germany*.
    Philadelphia: University of Pennsylvania Press.

King, Jr, Martin Luther. 1967. *The Trumpet of Conscience*. Boston:
    Beacon Press.

Kuber, W.N. 1987. *B.R. Ambedkar*. New Delhi: Ministry of Information
    and Broadcasting, Government of India.

Kumar, Aishwary. 2015. *Radical Equality: Ambedkar, Gandhi and the*
    *Risk of Democracy*. Stanford: Stanford University Press.

Landauer, Carl. 1989. 'Ortega Y Gasset and the Commitment of
    Ambivalence'. *Salmagundi*, no. 84 (Fall): 272–8.

Lerner, Robert. 1972. *The Heresy of the Free Spirit in the Later Middle*
    *Ages*. Berkeley: University of California Press.

Lokhande, G.S. 1977. *Bhimrao Ramli Ambedkar: A Study in Social*
    *Democracy*. New Delhi: Intellectual.

McGrath, Alister. 2010. *Heresy: A History of Defending the Truth*.
    London: Harper One.

Merleau-Ponty, Maurice. 1962 [1945]. *Phenomenology of Perception*, translated by Colin Smith. London and New York: Routledge and Kegan Paul.

Mishima, Yukio. 1958. *Confessions of a Mask*. New York: New Directions Books.

————. 1970. *Sun and Steel*, translated by John Bester. Tokyo: Kodansha International Ltd.

Montaigne, Michel de. 1870. *Essays of Seigneur de Montaigne*. London: Alex Murray & Son.

Mukherjee, Anuradha. 2015. 'Dr. B. R. Ambedkar's Critique of Mainstream Political Discourse'. In *Ambedkar and Social Justice: Legal, Political and Socio-economic Landscape*, edited by Sushama Yadav and Shri Prakash Singh. New Delhi: Manak Publications.

Mungekar, Bhalchandra. 2017. *The Essential Ambedkar*. New Delhi: Rupa Publications.

Narake, Hari, ed. 2003. *Dr. Babasaheb Ambedkar: Writings and Speeches*, Volume 17, Part 3. Mumbai: Education Department, Government of Maharashtra.

Nathan, John. 1974. *Mishima: A Biography*. Toronto: Little, Brown and Company.

Nietzsche, Friedrich. 2008. *Man Alone with Himself*. London: Penguin Books.

Ortega y Gasset, José. 1932. *The Revolt of the Masses*. London: W.W. Norton.

————. 1946. 'Notes on Thinking: Its Creation of the World and Its Creation of God. In *Concord and Liberty*, translated by Helene Weyl. New York: Publisher.

————. 1956. *The Dehumanization or Art and Other Writings*. New York: Doubleday.

————. 1963a. *Man and People*. New York: Norton Library.

————. 1963b. *Meditations on Quixote*. New York: Norton.

————. 2006. *Obras Completas*, Tomo IV: 1926–1931. Madrid: Taurus.

Ortega y Gasset, José, and Anthony Kerrigan. 1957. 'Morbid Democracy'. *Modern Age* (Winter): 53–6.

Pantham, Thomas. 2009. 'Against Untouchability: The Discourses of Gandhi and Ambedkar'. In *Humiliation: Claims and Context*, edited by Gopal Guru. New Delhi: Oxford University Press.

Pascal, Blaise. 1931. *Pensées*, translated by W.F. Trotter. New York: Everyman's Library.

———. 2013. *Thoughts*, selected and translated by Moritz Kaufmann. Cambridge: Cambridge University Press.

Rajasekhariah, A.M. 1989. *B.R. Ambedkar: The Quest for Social Justice*. New Delhi: Uppal.

Ramaiah, Avatthi, ed. 2017. *Contemporary Relevance of Ambedkar's Thoughts*. New Delhi: Rawat Publications.

Rodrigues, Valerian. 2002. *The Essential Writings of B.R. Ambedkar*. New Delhi: Oxford University Press.

Rogers, Kim W. 1994. 'Ortega and Ecological Philosophy'. *Journal of the History of Ideas* 55, no. 3 (July): 503–22.

———. 2003. *Reason and Life: An Introduction to an Ecological Approach in Philosophy*. Lanham: University Press of America.

Roy, Arundhati. 2019. *The Doctor and the Saint: The Ambedkar-Gandhi Debate: Caste, Race and Annihilation of Caste*. New Delhi: Penguin Random House India.

Saklofske, Donald H., Cecil R. Reynolds, and Vicki L. Schwean, eds. 2013. *The Oxford Handbook of Child Psychological Assessment*. Oxford: Oxford University Press.

Sakrikar, Dinkar. 1992. 'Dr. B.R. Ambedkar: The Leader of Social Regeneration'. In *Political Thinkers of India*, volume 16, edited by Verinder Grover. New Delhi: Deep and Deep Publications.

Schopenhauer, Arthur. 1970. *Essays and Aphorisms*. London: Penguin Classics.

———. 2012. *Life of Wisdom*. New York: Dover Publications.

Scott-Stokes, Henry. 1974. *The Life and Death of Yukio Mishima*. New York: Farrar, Straus and Giroux.

Seidensticker, Edward. 1971. 'Mishima Yukio'. *The Hudson Review* 24, no. 2 (Summer): 272–82.

Simmel, G. 1971. *On Individuality and Social Forms: Selected Writings*, edited and with an introduction by Donald N. Levine. Chicago: University of Chicago Press.

Simon, Walter Michael. 1972. *French Liberalism 1789–1848*. New York: Wiley & Sons.

Spinoza, Baruch. 2005. *Ethics*. New York: Barnes & Noble.

―――. 2009. *Theologico-political Treatise*. New York: Barnes & Noble.

Sprintzen, David. 1988. *Camus: A Critical Examination*. Philadelphia: Temple University Press.

Stokes, Henry Scott. 1974. *Life and Death of Yukio Mishima*. New York: Cooper Square Press.

Storey, John. 1997. *Cultural Theory and Popular Culture: An Introduction*. Athens: University of Georgia Press.

Vajpeyi, Ananya. 2012. *Righteous Republic: The Political Foundations of Modern India*. Boston: Harvard University Press.

Vlastos, Gregory. 1995. *Studies in Greek Philosophy*, volume 2, edited by Daniel W. Graham. Princeton: Princeton University Press.

Wagenaar, Dick, and Yoshio Iwamoto. 1975. 'Yukio Mishima: Dialectics of Mind and Body'. *Contemporary Literature* 16, no. 1 (Winter): 41–60.

Weil, Simone. 1986. *An Anthology*. London: Penguin Books.

Westler, Brendon, and Aurelian Craiutu. 2015. 'Two Critical Spectators: José Ortega y Gasset and Raymond Aron'. *The Review of Politics* 77, no. 4 (Fall): 575–602.

Willhoite, Jr, Fred H. 1961. 'Albert Camus' Politics of Rebellion'. *The Western Political Quarterly* 14, no. 2 (June): 400–14.

Yadav, Sushma, and Shri Prakash Singh, ed. 2015. *Ambedkar and Social Justice: Legal, Political and Socio-economic Landscape*. New Delhi: Manak Publications.

Yamanouchi, Hisaaki. 1972. 'Mishima Yukio and His Suicide'. *Modern Asian Studies* 6, no. 1: 1–16.

Zaretsky, Robert B. 2011. *Albert Camus: Elements of Life*. New York: Cornell University Press.

Zerner, Monique, ed. 1998. *Inventer l'Hérésie? Discours Polémiques et Pouvoirs avant l'Inquisition* (Inventing Heresy? Polemical Discourses and Powers before the Inquisition). Nice: Collection du Centre d'études médiévales de Nice.

# ABOUT THE AUTHOR

**Ramin Jahanbegloo** is a political philosopher. He is presently the executive director of the Mahatma Gandhi Center for Peace Studies and the vice dean of the Jindal Global Law School at O.P. Jindal Global University, Haryana, India. He is also a member of the advisory board of PEN Canada. He is the winner of the Peace Prize from the United Nations Association in Spain (2009) for his extensive academic works in promoting dialogue between cultures and his advocacy for non-violence, and, more recently, the Josep Palau i Fabre International Essay Prize. He has authored 32 books in English, French, and Persian. Among these are *Gadflies in the Public Space: A Socratic Legacy of Philosophical Dissent* (2016), *Letters to a Young Philosopher* (2018), *The Decline of Civilization: Why We Need to Return to Gandhi and Tagore* (2017), and *Albert Camus: The Unheroic Hero of Our Time* (2020).